T0246760

HAUNTED EASTERN WASHINGTON

DEBORAH CUYLE

HAunted
America

Published by Haunted America
A Division of The History Press
Charleston, SC
www.historypress.com

Copyright © 2024 by Deborah Cuyle
All rights reserved

First published 2024

Manufactured in the United States

ISBN 9781467157308

Library of Congress Control Number: 2024938198

Notice: The information in this book is true and complete to the best of our knowledge. It is offered without guarantee on the part of the author or The History Press. The author and The History Press disclaim all liability in connection with the use of this book.

All rights reserved. No part of this book may be reproduced or transmitted in any form whatsoever without prior written permission from the publisher except in the case of brief quotations embodied in critical articles and reviews.

I dedicate this book to all my friends, my family and the wonderful team at Arcadia Publishing and The History Press. My love of history, writing and haunted places is ultimately fueled by their continued interest and support as I travel my way through various states. I lived in Washington for several decades and have traveled to, lived in or enjoyed almost all the places in this book. I still relish my close relationships with dozens of people all across the state of Washington.

I am discovering that there are spirits everywhere—if we only take notice and pay attention to their small signals, their signs… their whispers. I seem to have several friendly spirits entertaining me in this old house. A tall, thin woman who wears a long, black dress: she casually paces back and forth through the front room. A cheerful gentleman who is very considerate and helpful: he manifests when I am sad, upset or otherwise stressed. A male jokester who likes to play games and move things around my house—just to keep things interesting…

So I dedicate this book to all the active and interesting ghosts out there. Without them, my books would not be possible!

CONTENTS

PREFACE

In this book, I explore new angles on hauntings, paranormal realms and mysterious places. Over the years, I have learned that there is so much more to the strange happenings we experience than just ghostly apparitions and things that go bump in the night. There are countless haunted places and events in Eastern Washington; it would have been hard to include them all, so I wrote about my favorites (and hopefully yours!).

As is common with my books, I have tried to incorporate as many historical facts, names and dates as possible into each chapter. This brings the ghosts and their stories to life and also makes learning about the different towns more interesting. I love hearing a good ghost story and then, on researching the building, actually being able to find evidence of someone with the same name as the spirit who actually lived there (or died there) at one time or another.

I have gone to great lengths to research as many specifics as possible for each of these stories. I hope to bring some forgotten pioneers and early Washington history back to life in the hearts and minds of my readers.

There are so many strange happenings in the world: bizarre phenomena and situations that defy all logic and fantastic places, monsters, unsolved mysteries and lost legends that both intrigue and delight us.

In this book, I address many unsolved murders and the restless spirits that are hanging around seeking justice or revenge or simply refusing to leave their favorite haunts. After poring over old newspapers for hours on end, I've

Above: Creepy, abandoned hallways are a perfect hiding spot for adventurous ghosts and misbehaved spirits! *Courtesy of Library of Congress (hereafter LOC) #2011636297, Carol M. Highsmith, photographer, Eastern State Penitentiary.*

Opposite: Washington's numerous ghost towns represent its fascinating history and offer excellent opportunities for paranormal investigations. *Courtesy of LOC #2018699003, Carol M. Highsmith, photographer, located in Thorp, WA.*

included some of the most bizarre true historical accounts from Washington's fascinating history. Other stories have been told to me by locals.

Within the walls of old buildings remains the residual energy needed to keep spirits restless and their stories alive—and, hopefully, their ghostly apparitions around.

The stories here are told out of fun, for the love of history, ghost stories, legends and lore. This book is not intended to be a nonfiction project, and even after hundreds of hours hunched over reading and researching, while I try to be as accurate as possible, I still find conflicting dates, misspelled names and inconsistent historic details—so please take this book for what it is.

As you pore through these pages, stop and take the time to learn more about Eastern Washington's early settlers and pioneers—the ones who blazed their way across the open plains to reach fertile soil and beautiful rivers to make their homestead claims.

So settle in with a nice cup of coffee or a glass of wine and discover tales of many mischievous ghosts, fascinating legends and the interesting history of *Haunted Eastern Washington*.

Enjoy!

ACKNOWLEDGEMENTS

There are many people to thank for this endeavor, and without their help and guidance, this book would not have been possible. My wonderful Washington books editor, Laurie Krill, is always such a pleasure to work with, along with all the other incredible people at Arcadia Publishing and The History Press. Their enthusiasm for their mission to promote local history is infectious, and I am blessed to work on my books with them. Their dedication to recording local history is nothing less than amazing, and without them, many books would never have been written.

And as always, I want to thank every single person who does what they can to preserve history. In this fast-paced and high-tech world, the past can, unfortunately, be forgotten, and every effort to maintain and record valuable data, photographs, diaries, documents and records is of the utmost importance for future generations.

One final request: please do not disturb or trespass on any of the locations listed throughout this book. Before exploring or investigating any of these locations, please acquire permission from the relevant property or business owners. Thank you for your understanding.

INTRODUCTION

Now I know what a ghost is. Unfinished business, that's what.
—*Salman Rushdie,* The Satanic Verses

What is a ghost? What is a haunting? And why do these things continue to both excite and frighten us?

The fascinating and spooky world of phantoms and spirits intrigues us all. We love unexplained events, dark apparitions, objects that mysteriously move on their own and the creepy sounds of disembodied voices and footsteps.

It is believed that ghosts are the "confused dead." For some reason, they do not understand they are dead and thus wander around restlessly. Ghosts may also cling to the earthly world because they need something resolved. Was their killer captured and sentenced for the crime? Is there a valuable item or money that the ghost wants to make sure gets into the right hands? Or were their possessions distributed in a manner that went against their final wishes? Ghosts linger for many reasons.

In *Haunted Eastern Washington*, we will explore a large variety of paranormal activities, gruesome true crimes, creepy happenings, unexplained events, legends, lore and so much more. I hope the stories in these pages make the hair on the back of your neck stand up, followed by a faint whisper from someone unseen or maybe even the touch of an invisible hand upon your shoulder…

The mysteries of the paranormal world have intrigued people for centuries. *Courtesy of LOC #2022647929, Melander & Bro., Publisher, 1874.*

HAUNTED EASTERN WASHINGTON

Eastern Washington is the region of Washington State located east of the beautiful Cascade mountain range. It contains the wonderful city of Spokane (the second-largest city in the state), the Tri-Cities (Kennewick, Pasco, and Richland), the Columbia River, the massive Grand Coulee Dam, the Hanford Nuclear Reservation and the fertile farmlands of the Yakima Valley and the Palouse. This region is more sparce than its western half of Washington, which includes large cities like Seattle and Tacoma.

Many consider Eastern Washington the most picturesque part of the state—and also the most haunted!

CHAPTER 1
UPPER EASTERN REGION

WENATCHEE TO SPOKANE
AND EVERYWHERE ABOVE

Maybe all the people who say ghosts don't exist are just afraid to admit that they do.
—Michael Ende, The Neverending Story

WENATCHEE

The area now known as Wenatchee was once inhabited by the Wenatchi tribe. They lived harmoniously with nature, relying mostly on salmon, plant roots, local berries and nuts to survive. Once word got out about the area's extremely fertile land, many settlers—gold miners, missionaries, cattle ranchers and Chinese immigrants—started making their way to Wenatchee.

Well-known Wenatchee businessman Samuel Miller was born in 1829 in Peoria, Illinois, and died 1906 at age seventy-seven. Later in life, Miller's adventurous spirit led him to northern Arizona, where gold fever gripped many minds. He eventually found his way back to Washington Territory, where he decided to lay down roots and became the first postmaster (of what would later become Wenatchee) in 1884 and worked as such until 1890.

Formally platted in 1888, Wenatchee was officially founded by Don Carlos Corbett (1855–1927, age seventy-two), a member of a Seattle law firm. His legal expertise helped facilitate many land transactions, various property plats and other processes necessary for the town's growth.

In 1898, the Wenatchee Fire Department (WFD) was seventeen men. L.O. Hall was chief, and George Evans, Dr. Gilchrist, William Cummings and Percy Schebley were the most active members. Pictured: the WFD Chemical No. 1 in 1911. *Courtesy of LOC #2007678209.*

Wenatchee Avenue in downtown Wenatchee, looking south from First Street, 1912. *Courtesy of Spokane Public Library (hereafter SPL) #5601.*

In 1892, the Great Northern Railway decided to build a train depot about a mile south of Wenatchee, leading to increased population and travel. Soon, the town was bustling with three hundred citizens. The arrival of the railroad brought a new "rough element" into town. Drunkenness, prostitution, disorderly behavior and crimes ranging from petty theft to murder became more common. To cater to the scoundrels, within just one block there were thirteen dance halls and multiple saloons.

Today, Wenatchee is home to over thirty-five thousand residents, and the area is known for its glorious apple farms—it is considered the "Apple Capital of the World." But beautiful Wenatchee also has a more mysterious and dark side. Legends of various ghosts and unexplained phenomena are favorite stories to be told around the campfire…

PROP MAN GHOST OF MISSION RIDGE

An active ghost named the Prop Man has haunted Mission Ridge ever since 1944, when the U.S. B-24 bomber *Liberator*, carrying six crew members, tragically crashed into the side of the mountain.

On a dark, windy and stormy night—September 30, 1944—Flight 22 out of the Walla Walla Army Air Base wandered off course due to the severe weather conditions. High above the Cascade mountains, the *Liberator* was on a routine training mission; however, the fog was dense, and the pilots were having trouble seeing anything. Unfortunately for the Flight 22 crew, what exactly happened that night is unknown. The absence of advanced recording technology (such as cockpit voice recorders or flight data recorders) during that era meant that after the crash, written reports were compiled by interviewing eyewitness and examining physical evidence to determine what transpired during the ill-fated flight.

Men at the local Beehive Lookout reported hearing the sound of a "plane flying low" at eight o'clock that night. Just minutes later, the *Liberator* tragically crashed into the mountain about five hundred feet below the crest of Mission Ridge. The lookout team witnessed the horrifying sight of a fire as the plane exploded.

To make matters worse, the rain was torrential, and rescue efforts were delayed until the morning, as it would have been extremely difficult to get to the area of the accident. Trekking up the side of a steep, uncharted mountain by horseback in the mud and rain would have been an extremely challenging task. (Remember, in 1944, helicopters were not yet common and

Above: In 1944, a B-24 Liberator like this one lost control and crashed into Mission Ridge. There were no survivors. One of the crew now haunts the ski slopes. *Courtesy of LOC #2002722136.*

Opposite: The incredible Cascade Mountains are as beautiful as they are mysterious and dangerous. *Courtesy of LOC, #2011630306, Carol M. Highsmith, photographer.*

were still in their preliminary stages of development. While the concept of vertical flight had been explored, practical and operational helicopters were not widely used at that time.)

The *Liberator* was a massive plane, weighing sixty-five thousand pounds and carrying ten .50-caliber machine guns. When the rescue team finally made their way to the crash site, they were solemn. No crew members had survived. Their bodies were carefully removed and brought to town, along with various pieces of the wreck. The ten machine guns were also loaded onto horses and brought back to town. As the funerals of the young men proceeded, townspeople, family members and friends mourned their loss.

The tragic deaths of these brave young men must be remembered and honored, their names never to be forgotten.

Since the crash, skiers and snowboarders have repeatedly seen the spirit of one of the young aviators roaming the slopes. His apparition is often seen with the ghostly image of the plane's prop nearby. Perhaps he is searching for his fellow crew members who died with him in the tragedy? No one knows why his restless spirit lingers amid the snow. Many employees and personnel working at the ski lodge have experienced the Prop Man ghost, too.

A memorial stands on the mountain honoring these six men. A twelve-foot section of the *Liberator*'s wing was scavenged from the crash site and relocated as a remembrance. A waymark plaque (a marker or sign that designates a unique location) with more information about the crash is also available to view.

The honorable young men who tragically lost their lives were:

Second Lieutenant James D. Hunt (1922–1944, age twenty-one), pilot
Flight Officer Robert J. Hennekes (1924–1944, age nineteen), navigator
Second Lieutenant Ted Ray Lewis (1923–1944, age twenty), co-pilot
Corporal Calvin Dean Flaming (1924–1944, age twenty), gunner
Corporal James R. Manthei (1919–1944, age twenty-five), radio operator
Second Lieutenant Francis William Lequier (1922–1944, age twenty-two), bombardier

NOTE: The memorial is reached by skiing down from the top of chair 2 at Mission Ridge Ski Area and going down the ski run Bomber Bowl.

World War II, the deadliest military conflict in history so far, resulted in an estimated total of seventy to eighty-five million people who perished during the horrendous conflict.

EAST WENATCHEE CEMETERY

Among the tombstones and historic trees in the East Wenatchee Cemetery, eerie tales of ghostly apparitions wandering among the graves unfold. There are reportedly three spirits haunting the graveyard, all beckoning for interaction with the living.

The East Wenatchee Cemetery, also known as the Evergreen Memorial Park, has a rich history in Wenatchee Valley. The first recorded burial in the cemetery was that of Leila Shugart, who passed away in February 1872.

The ghosts that linger in the cemetery are a bit of an unsolved mystery. The first is a curious spirit, the ghost of a former soldier. Many people have spotted this spirit wearing full uniform, wandering the grounds as if searching for something. Who is this lost soldier? What is he looking for? Nobody knows. The cemetery is home to many Civil War veterans, as well as men who fought in World Wars I and II. There are even soldiers who served during the Korean War and the Vietnam War buried there—so there is really no way of telling who the Ghost Soldier is.

Some visitors also report seeing the spirit of a veiled woman wandering the cemetery, her eyes filled with sorrow. Perhaps she is the wife of someone buried in the cemetery? Perhaps she is the mother of a child buried there and is mourning her loss? No one knows who the sad woman is, but maybe someday she can cross over to the other side and find peace.

More questions than answers surround the ghosts that linger at the East Wenatchee Cemetery.

NOTE: The East Wenatchee cemetery is located at 1301 Tenth Street Northeast, East Wenatchee, Washington 98802.

THE GHOSTS OF ISABELLA AND ELIJAH AT THE WENATCHEE VALLEY MUSEUM & CULTURAL CENTER

The Wenatchee Valley Museum & Cultural Center, with its winding corridors and hidden chambers, has long been the subject of whispered tales of ghosts. Visitors, both curious and apprehensive, have shared their eerie encounters when asked.

The story goes that a long time ago, in the museum's dimly lit archives, an old curator named Elijah Thorne once presided. His passion for preserving history bordered on obsession, and he guarded the artifacts as if they held the most intimate of secrets.

One moonless night, as the clock struck midnight, Elijah sensed a strange presence in the room with him. The air thickened, and shadows danced across old manuscripts and books. He glimpsed a shadowy figure—a woman in a long gown?—drifting slowly through the exhibit halls.

Elijah (who was secretly mesmerized by her beauty) believed the woman was a local musician named Ms. Isabella. Her ghost wore an elegant gown of celestial blue fabric, and her seductive eyes were captivating. She barely made a sound as her feather-light footsteps echoed in the dark halls and onto the stairways. Her apparition moved most gracefully but never seemed to notice poor Elijah.

One evening, Isabella lingered near the antique piano, her fingers ever so lightly brushing the keys. For when she was alive, she was a pianist, and her musical talent left people breathless. Local legend says that one day, she composed a haunting and sad sonata—a song about lost love. She was hopelessly and madly in love with a man in town and could think of no other. But tragedy struck—her lover mysteriously vanished without an explanation, leaving only a single blue rose on her doorstep. Isabella's heart was broken forever.

While alone one night, Elijah spotted the spirit of the beautiful Isabella once more as she casually wandered around the museum. Room by room, she charmingly moved with only the slightest sound, her long gown trailing behind her. He eagerly followed her, transfixed by her elegant splendor.

In one of the back rooms, Isabella suddenly stopped and seemed to be searching for something. Elijah carefully peeked around the corner, eager to see what his fair lady was up to. Then, in the blink of an eye, she mysteriously vanished into thin air! Elijah was left shocked and bewildered. The haunting event troubled Elijah for the rest of his days, uncertain as he was of Ms. Isabella's fate.

Visitors claim to hear Isabella's beautiful sonata, especially near the piano on stormy nights. Some say Elijah, too, became part of the museum after he died, forever searching for his lovely Isabella.

NOTE: The Wenatchee Valley Museum & Cultural Center is located at 127 South Mission Street, Wenatchee, Washington 98801. Journey through the museum's creepy underground hallways, intricate mazes, secret passageways and several themed rooms that rival scenes from Hollywood horror classics. Its annual Haunted Museum event opens nightly at six o'clock on the last couple weeks of October. Call for schedule and dates: (509) 888-6240. This attraction contains bright flashing lights, lasers, fog machines, scent devices, loud noises, startle effects, confined spaces, eerie stairs, spooky dark areas— and lots of guaranteed frightful fun!

MOUNT RAINIER UFOS

What other unusual and unexplained phenomena can haunt us? Do all scary things have to revolve around ghostly apparitions or disembodied voices and phantom footsteps? The answer is no. Many strange things can create fear within us. Anything that cannot be logically explained can induce panic and terror within the mind. One such ongoing mystery is the appearance of unidentified flying objects (UFOs).

The very first recorded UFO sighting was written down as far back as March 1, 1639, by a Puritan and governor of the Massachusetts Bay Colony named John Winthrop. As Winthrop and his men were sailing on the ocean, they looked up toward the skies and were shocked by what they witnessed.

The first officially documented UFO sighting in the United States was by experienced pilot Kenneth Arnold over Mount Rainier in Eastern Washington (pictured here) on June 24, 1947. *Courtesy of Seattle Public Library.*

Winthrop wrote in his daily log that the "strange object darted back and forth through the sky and emitted flames and sparkles." He also noted another bizarre phenomenon: somehow, their boat had effortlessly traveled a great distance *against* the strong tide! Winthrop and his crew were not the only ones to observe this flying object, as many other credible witnesses also saw the strange aircraft. Since air travel did not exist in 1639, what was the shining object that traveled so swiftly in the sky? Were the men abducted by aliens, making this the first known report of an abduction, too? How did all the men have no recollection whatsoever of rowing their boat the long mile it would have taken to arrive at their location?

Then, 308 years later, another man was stupefied by strange objects in the sky. One of the first officially documented UFO sightings in the United States was near Mount Rainier in Eastern Washington on June 24, 1947, by experienced Idaho bush pilot Kenneth Arnold. Arnold reported seeing a "formation of nine unusual, shiny objects that he believed were traveling at speeds of 1,200 miles per hour." His description of the objects' shape, often described as "saucerlike," contributed to the popularization of the new term *flying saucer*.

In 1947, the fastest aircraft was the Bell X–1, which was the first aircraft to officially break the sound barrier. It was piloted by Chuck Yeager on October

14, 1947, and reached a speed of Mach 1.06, or 807.2 miles per hour. So if the very credible and experienced pilot Arnold was calculating correctly, these spaceships were traveling almost twice as fast!

That day, Arnold was en route from Chehalis to Yakima for a leisurely business trip. Always adventurous, he had heard of a $5,000 reward for the location of the U.S. Marine Corps R5C that crashed on December 10, 1946, en route from San Diego to Seattle. The airplane crashed near the South Tahoma Glacier on the side of Mount Rainier, tragically killing all thirty-two U.S. marines on board. The R5C pilot was flying entirely by instruments in the severe weather, and it was determined that wind had moved the aircraft off course.

As Arnold made his flight, he hoped he could spot some of the debris and not only help the families of the marines get closure but also get a hefty reward (the equivalent of approximately $57,497.87 in today's money). But as he searched below, disappointingly, he saw no evidence of the crash. Somewhere over Mineral Lake, around three o'clock in the afternoon, Arnold gave up on his $5,000 reward idea, ventured back onto his original flight course and continued on his route. He had not spotted any evidence of the crash and needed to mind his fuel level.

The R5C wreckage was finally found in July 1947. The bodies of the thirty-two U.S. marines were found high on the face of the glacier, but hazardous conditions forced authorities to abandon plans to remove them for burial. Sadly, the marines will remain entombed forever on Mount Rainier.

Now back on track, Arnold soon experienced an event that would change his life forever. He suddenly noticed a cluster of nine shiny crafts traveling beside him. Ruling out all logical explanations, he was left bewildered and startled by the strange objects. But after a few minutes, they swiftly jetted away off toward Mount Adams (about fifty miles south of Mount Rainier) at lightning speed, leaving Arnold scratching his head, completely puzzled and shocked.

When Arnold landed his plane in Yakima, he told his pilot friends what he had experienced just a few hours earlier. They urged him to tell his story to the press. They knew Arnold was a credible witness and a level-headed man.

But soon after Arnold told reporters about the UFOs to reporters, skeptics immediately began ridiculing him. This did not deter Arnold. He knew what he had seen, and luckily, other witnesses soon reported having seen the UFOs near Yakima. Even more reliable was the fact that an entire United Airlines flight crew flying over Idaho en route to Seattle that day also reported seeing five to nine disklike objects that followed their plane for fifteen minutes before suddenly disappearing.

On November 18, 1957, Arnold was quoted in the *Spokane Chronicle* as saying:

> *I have closely watched the reports of unidentified flying objects for 10 years. I have seen them myself on five more occasions since my original sighting. I have even photographed these objects. I'm certain we are not alone in the atmosphere and in spite of official denials, I am equally certain that the Air Force is aware of this.*

Countless UFO sightings have been reported since Arnold's testimony. Some of the reports are typical, and other reports are downright frightening. Until there is hard evidence, UFO stories will continue to haunt and fascinate people all around the world. Yet Arnold's exciting experience would soon take a back seat to one of the most notorious UFO crashes in history: the notorious Roswell UFO incident that occurred one month later, on July 8, 1947…

LEAVENWORTH

Of all the places I have visited and enjoyed hanging out in, Leavenworth has got to be one of my top ten favorites. This incredibly beautiful town is nestled just outside of the picturesque Cascade Range and never ceases to dazzle and amaze the millions of visitors it welcomes each year. One trip to Leavenworth and you will be hooked for life, making it a new destination to explore time and again. If you're intrigued by quirky and fascinating collections, head to the Leavenworth Nutcracker Museum and discover an extensive assortment of nutcrackers from various cultures and time periods. The museum provides insights into the history and craftsmanship of these whimsical devices.

Leavenworth's downtown area is a charming Bavarian-style village, complete with cobblestone streets, half-timbered buildings and colorful flower boxes. Explore boutique shops, art galleries and specialty stores, and don't miss the chance to savor authentic German cuisine at local restaurants. Outdoor enthusiasts will love Peshastin Pinnacles, a unique state park known

The beautiful Bavarian-themed town of Leavenworth has multiple haunted buildings and, it is rumored, many ghosts. *Courtesy of author.*

for its towering rock formations, excellent hiking trails and rock-climbing opportunities. Beyond Peshastin Pinnacles, Leavenworth offers many rafting and mountain biking opportunities. Explore nearby trails in the Alpine Lakes Wilderness or along Icicle Creek. In winter, enjoy cross-country skiing and snowshoeing in the snow-covered landscapes. If you wish to enjoy wine tasting, Leavenworth is also part of the Cascade Valley Wine Country. The town hosts a variety of festivals throughout the year, including the famous Leavenworth Oktoberfest (modeled after the original Munich celebration). Other events include the Christmas Lighting Festival and the Bavarian Ice Festival. There is always something fun to do at Leavenworth any time of the year.

The town of Leavenworth was originally called Icicle Flats and was first settled as a trading post. The area was home to several tribes, the Yakama, Chinook and Wenatchi, who hunted deer and elk and fished for salmon in the nearby Icicle Creek. Soon, more settlers arrived in the area in search of gold, timber and furs, and by 1890, Icicle Flats was born. Next, the arrival of the railroad brought an influx of people to the area, and the logging and sawmill industry boomed along with it. However, when the railroad was rerouted and moved out of Leavenworth, it almost turned into a ghost town.

But Leavenworth refused to vanish. In the 1960s, the town leaders brainstormed and produced an ingenious idea: to completely change Leavenworth's appearance. They slowly renovated almost every building downtown, creating a unique and colorful Bavarian village theme. Bright murals adorned almost every shop, and German-style decor cropped up everywhere. Next, they created a series of fun festivals and events that soon began drawing tourists into town.

Today, the bustling town is packed every day with people enjoying walking the streets, shopping and eating amazing meals, and it draws millions of visitors every year. Make Leavenworth one of your next destinations—you will not be sorry!

And while you're enjoying local activities, perhaps you can spot a ghost or two! Leavenworth has several resident spirits who refuse to leave the buildings in which they eternally linger.

THE OLD TUMWATER INN RESTAURANT & LOUNGE BUILDING

A local favorite, the Tumwater Inn offered more than simply great food and amazing drinks for several decades: live music and fun events were also featured at the historic hangout. Considered one of the oldest restaurants in Leavenworth, it is no wonder the building has its very own ghosts.

The Tumwater spirit likes to move objects around, play games on unsuspecting people and even impress everyone with a paranormal tune on the piano that was built in 1871! Some believe the ghost of a young girl is practicing at the piano keys.

The spirit of an older gentleman can also be seen throughout the building, most often in the kitchen areas. Is this a ghost chef? A waiter who refuses to leave his old job? Or perhaps the male entity is simply a prior customer who thinks of the Tumwater as his eternal happy place? Some like to think the gentleman is the spirit of Harry Osbourne, a local favorite owner of the building, who loved to entertain the ladies.

The original kitchen opened its doors in 1911 as the Overland Café, run by proprietor John Tabuchi. Soon, Harry Osbourne took charge of the café and changed its name to the Osbourne Café. Harry loved to entertain the local ladies with fancy tea parties. Women would dress up in their best attire and come to the café to be pampered exquisitely and told how beautiful

The old Tumwater Inn building has reportedly been haunted by a couple ghosts for several decades. *Courtesy of author.*

they looked by Harry. He soon became fabulously popular with the ladies in town. In the evenings, Harry would entertain his guests after a nice meal with local musicians, and everyone would dance the night away.

The café changed hands and names several more times over the next few years. In 1922, an ambitious lady named Emma Anderson bought the café and renamed it the Tumwater Gateway Café.

Sandy Owens-Carmody participated in running the Tumwater Inn Restaurant and Lounge in Leavenworth for thirty years. She co-owned the restaurant, which had been a part of Leavenworth's history through the 1940s, '50s and '60s. Unfortunately, the restaurant closed its doors in July 2017 after new building owners took over the property and decided not to renew the lease. Sandy and her husband, Charlie, faced unexpected challenges, and despite their efforts, they were unable to continue operating the beloved establishment. The Tumwater Inn held many cherished memories for those who frequented it over the years. Sandy welcomed her ghosts and enjoyed the silly games they played on her, like rearranging the condiments in the middle of the night.

Since then, the building has changed hands once again and is Tumwater Bread & Pizza as of this writing. Hopefully, the newest proprietor will enjoy the company of the friendly ghosts as much as the previous owners did!

NOTE: The old Tumwater building is located at 219 Ninth Street, Leavenworth, Washington 98226.

THE OLD EDELWEISS HOTEL (THE LOFT BAR & GRILL)

This building was constructed in 1906 and was once even a brothel! Later it was called the Chikamin Hotel. The main level has hosted several shops, and the Edelweiss Hotel was once located upstairs.

Multiple mischievous ghosts like to turn lights on and off and move objects around in the middle of the night. A female spirit wearing a Victorian-style dress is often seen in the upstairs windows, looking down over the street below. Who was she? Why does her spirit linger at this spot? Was she a former landlady, a lady of ill repute or perhaps the wife of someone who once lived there? No one knows.

Sometimes the sound of faint arguing comes through the walls when no one is nearby. Who is this phantom couple seeking to reconcile a mysterious dispute from the past?

Downstairs, the ghosts of a phantom couple can be seen at times. Are these the same ghosts that can be heard arguing upstairs? Some claim the male entity involved is a man named George.

The beautiful building was the brainstorm of early Icicle Flats pioneer Frank Losekamp, who moved to the Icicle area in 1891. In 1906, Losekamp had tons of bricks hauled to town to construct his two-story Losekamp Building at 843 Front Street, which soon housed the Tumwater Bank Savings and Bank, the L.D. Company and Losekamp's store. Losekamp was the first person to open a general store in the area. He had the grueling task of bringing supplies and goods to Icicle from Ellensburg, Washington, loaded in packs on the backs of his mules. He also built the very first log cabin in the area—a mere ten feet by ten feet in size but a small luxury for the time. The never-tiring man also became the town's first postmaster, solely in charge of sorting and organizing the mail that would arrive twice a week by stagecoach. During the early Icicle years, the town was just a few crude shacks and a muddy street (where Waterfront Park is currently located).

In 1906, Losekamp rented the upper half of the building on a five-year lease to a couple from Alaska, Mr. and Mrs. Ed Westbrook. The couple wished to open a fancy hotel, which soon came to be called the Hotel Franklin. But the endeavor would only last a year. Business dealings would force the Westbrooks to return to Alaska. In 1907, the Westbrooks sold their interest in the hotel to Ira G. Farmer.

Farmer came from Wenatchee and in 1903 worked at the Lamb-Davis Lumber Company in town. In 1905, he was employed at Tumwater Savings and Bank. In 1907, he worked at the Tumwater Light & Water Company until he decided to take the leap and become the proprietor of the Hotel Franklin. (In 1907, the Tumwater Bank Savings and Bank was located on the ground level of the Losekamp Building.) He enjoyed several years at the Hotel Franklin until he sold his interest to George Godfrey. Farmer would go on to Bremerton, Washington, and was working in the navy yard in 1909.

Godfrey had spent the last few years working as a cashier and express agent in Leavenworth until he accepted the task of running the Hotel Franklin. Is his the ghost that haunts the hotel? Why would George Godfrey remain in the building after his death? Another paranormal mystery.

The building has changed hands and names multiple times over the years, but the ghosts have stayed put where they continue to live to this day.

NOTE: The building located at 843 Front Street, Leavenworth, Washington. The former Loft evolved and moved into its current location at 843 Front Street after a grueling remodel of the upstairs space in the Edelweiss building. The work was done by friends, family and even the owners themselves. The Loft continues to prioritize quality food and drinks and an enthusiastic, welcoming atmosphere for visitors.

LEAVENWORTH CEMETERY

Nothing is more frightening than a cemetery late at night! And the graveyard in Leavenworth is especially scary.

The ghost of a small girl can be seen occasionally, both night and day.

In 1916, a local man named John Phillips retold a ghost story that was printed in the *Leavenworth Echo*. He was fishing when he heard a faint *choo choo* of a train—but there was no train! John had heard rumors of a ghost train but had never experienced it for himself. A real train had had the misfortune of heading onto a collapsed bridge and went tumbling down and crashed into the freezing waters below.

The sound of the ghost train subsided, and John suddenly noticed a small girl standing alone in the water. Curiously, she started laughing.

"How can you laugh?" he asked her.

"I am the spirit of the one who years ago went down with that train and died," she informed him.

Astonished, John froze and did not know how to respond.

Then the girl looked at him again and said, "Carry me yonder to the bank so from there I may go back to my resting place in the cemetery."

Other people have claimed to see old-style railway lanterns lighting up the night air—swinging casually from invisible hands! Some paranormal investigators believe these restless spirits are those of railroad workers who died on the job and are buried in the graveyard. Sometimes, late at night, the sounds of railroad spikes being pounded into the hard ground can be heard, complemented by phantom men whistling while they work.

NOTE: To learn more about Leavenworth's fascinating paranormal events and get more detailed information about the town's incredible history, please read *Ghosts of Leavenworth and the Cascade Foothills* by Deborah Cuyle, published by The History Press.

THE WELLINGTON DISASTER OF 1910

THE GHOSTS IN THE RAVINE

The worst combination avalanche/train wreck in United States history occurred on March 1, 1910, killing over one hundred people within seconds. And the victims still haunt the ravine where their lives were tragically taken over 114 years ago on a drizzly, freezing night.

Nestled in a remote town called Wellington, a handful of people made their living catering to Great Northern Railroad (GNRR) crews and occasional tourists. Wellington no longer exists, but the residual energy from that fateful night and all those who lost their lives lingers on in the form of apparitions, disembodied voices and eerie sounds.

Some claim to have heard far-off screams, the screeching of train brakes and the faint sounds of thunder and lightning when the skies are clear. There are no trains running on the tracks to Wellington anymore, so from where do these sounds originate? Can a major catastrophe, taking the lives of so many, be woven into into the fabric of the supernatural for eternity? Many paranormal investigators believe so.

That week, the Great Northern Spokane Local No. 25 and the Fast Mail No. 27 slowly climbed their way into the Cascade mountain range, far from the safety of the town of Leavenworth. The innocent crew and passengers had no idea most of them would be dead in just a few days.

The snowfall was so extreme that the rotary plows could not keep up. As soon as the tracks were clear, another tumble of snow would cover them, making them impassible once again. In some places, the snow was thirty feet deep. For six long days, the trains were trapped in heavy blizzard and avalanche conditions. To make matters worse, on February 26, the telegraph lines went down, and communication with the outside was now lost. There was now no way to call for help if needed.

While passengers thought they were safe in the trains, they had no idea the cars were situated in a death trap. Bailet's Hotel proprietor William R. Bailet had told GNRR engineers just a few days before the accident that in all his eighteen years at Wellington, there had never been an avalanche on the spot where the trains were parked.

But in the middle of the night, a large lightning bolt struck the top of the mountain, causing two football fields' worth of built-up snow to come crashing down the hillside. The ginormous avalanche roared down Windy Mountain near Stevens Pass, causing death and destruction in its path.

Within seconds, all fourteen train cars were shoved down into the ravine above Tye Creek, killing almost everyone on board.

Charles Andrews, a Great Northern employee, witnessed the actual avalanche disaster:

> *White Death went moving down the mountainside above the trains. Relentlessly it advanced, exploding, roaring, rumbling, grinding, snapping—a crescendo of sound that might have been the crashing of ten thousand freight trains. It descended to the ledge where the sidetracks lay, picked up cars and equipment as though they were so many snow-draped toys, and swallowing them up, disappeared like a white, broad monster into the ravine below.*

Rescue efforts started immediately, but the results were grim. Charles Andrew and many Wellington residents rushed to the crushed trains that lay 150 feet below the railroad tracks. The rescue team managed to rescue twenty-three people, many of whom were injured. Sometimes they uncovered a half-frozen person, relieved to be alive. The survivors were found buried under 40 feet of freezing snow after the train coaches rolled nearly one thousand feet down the slope.

Volunteers had to follow trails of blood to locate bodies. They poked long sticks down into the snow in a gruesome search for solid objects. For days, in the freezing cold, they slowly dug up bodies, one by one, from under the many tons of snow. Then they dragged the bodies on sleds for miles until they could be hoisted down a slope to nearby Scenic. The grisly task included tying ropes to the victims' feet and lowering the bodies headfirst to the men below, where the bodies would be loaded onto a train to be shipped off once the tracks were clear.

But because Wellington was so remote and the railroad tracks were closed, no outside rescue efforts were readily unavailable. Brave people walked from nearby Scenic to help search for survivors and wrap and tag the bodies. A makeshift morgue and hospital were created from bunkhouses and spare buildings.

Many of the bodies of the railroad workers that were sleeping in the cars would remain unidentified (numerous workers could not speak English and signed their time cards simply with an *X*) and were eventually buried in a mass grave in Everett, Washington, courtesy of the Great Northern Railroad.

The tragedy would change the small town of Wellington forever.

A plaque memorializing the victims of the Wellington tragedy is down in the ravine where the trains landed and the bodies were discovered. *Courtesy of author.*

Years later, the Great Northern rerouted, and Wellington dried up and became a ghost town. The Boy Scouts of America used the site for years, but eventually, the historic buildings were demolished and most of the evidence of what once was has, sadly, disappeared.

Many people who have visited the former Wellington site have reported feelings of sadness, the echoes of disembodied voices, phantom footsteps inside the concrete snowshed and the eerie sounds of trains passing by. (Trains can no longer run on the tracks because they are closed off.) It is said that some people and dogs refuse to even go inside the snowshed for unexplained reasons. Dogs often bark at unseen people or things until they are pulled away by their owners and back to the safety of their automobiles.

NOTE: The author has experienced much unexplained paranormal activity while visiting the site of the accident. While alone in the ravine, she placed a tape recorder on one of the large tree trunks (still scarred from one of the trains crashing onto it—like deep, long cat scratches running the length of

People exploring the abandoned Cascade Tunnel at the Wellington avalanche site have reported seeing lanterns and hearing voices coming from deep inside. *Courtesy of author.*

the huge tree). Once back in the safety of her car, she played back the tape recorder. Shockingly, she heard the voices of dozens of ghosts. It sounded like being in a crowded room with multiple people talking over each other at the same time. This was the most convincing and confounding evidence ever experienced by the author. There is no logical explanation for this occurrence, as she was completely alone in the ravine. The site is extremely remote, almost impossible to find unless one is educated in history and privy to the location. Only the old snowshed, the Iron Goat Trail and the crumbling Cascade Tunnel remain, along with a few rusty relics still littering the hard-to-reach ravine.

A HAUNTED SNOWSHED

The old snowshed erected after the Wellington disaster seems to hold strange forces within its dark concrete walls. The eerie feeling of being followed when walking inside the shed is almost unbearable.

Visitors hear phantom voices, and dogs refuse to enter the concrete snowshed at Wellington. Many believe it is haunted. *Courtesy of author.*

Could the energy from the disaster have trapped its victims at the site for all eternity? Perhaps the eerie voices people hear are the ghosts of those deceased victims? Many visitors hear disembodied voices inside the old snowshed—the echoes of those silenced by the avalanche.

To safeguard trains from future avalanches, the Great Northern Railway constructed snowsheds over the nine miles of tracks between Scenic and Tye. These snowsheds were designed to prevent snow from drifting over the tracks during heavy snowfall and avalanche conditions. The Great Northern built a 2,463-foot-long double-track snowshed. This impressive structure was nearly half a mile in length and provided essential protection for passing trains. Due to the high cost of construction, this snowshed was unique, as it was the only all-concrete snowshed ever built by the Great Northern Railway. The decision to use concrete demonstrated the company's commitment to safety and preventing future disasters.

In addition to the snowsheds, the Great Northern Railway opened the New Cascade Tunnel in 1929. This tunnel bypassed Wellington altogether and provided a safer route through the Cascade mountains. The new tunnel was a significant engineering feat and remains the longest railroad tunnel in the United States.

Perhaps visit the site one day yourself and see if you experience anything strange. If you are brave enough to trek down the ravine to the actual site, you will notice a plaque memorializing the tragedy. Fragments of broken glass, long coils of steam pipes, miscellaneous hunks of rusty metal—all testify to the hundred-plus people who lost their lives that tragic day in 1910.

NOTE: To learn more about this tragic but fascinating Pacific Northwest catastrophe, please read *The 1910 Wellington Disaster* by Deborah Cuyle from Arcadia Publishing. This well-researched book includes a complete list of the victims and pictures of the people involved in the tragedy. The old Wellington site has been preserved as part of the Iron Goat Trail, which is accessible from US Highway 2 near Stevens Pass or near Scenic, east of Everett. There is a small sign that reads, "Wellington," but the road is only accessible for part of the year due to weather conditions. The original Cascade Tunnel is closed due to dangerous conditions like falling rocks and flooding. Please do not enter.

CHELAN

Lake Chelan, around which the city of Chelan is nestled, was slowly formed from a glacier valley over ten thousand years ago. The Cascade mountains also shaped Lake Chelan as glaciers drained into its basin. The original inhabitants of the Chelan area were the Salish-speaking Chelan tribe. These early Chelan people adopted elements of the Plains Indian culture, including their local styles of dress, beautiful beadwork and excellent horse-riding abilities.

Today, the charming town of Chelan offers a blend of fun outdoor activities, fantastic local cuisine, great shopping and an abundance of culture. Currently around 4,470 people consider beautiful Chelan their home.

One can also explore the more than thirty wineries in the Lake Chelan Valley, known for their award-winning wines. So whether you visit in summer or winter, Lake Chelan has something for everyone—everything from hiking and boating to skiing and wine tasting.

But there are also more mysterious and unusual aspects of this incredible town. Lingering stories of haunted old buildings and creepy lake creatures have been passed down for decades.

THE RUBY THEATRE

The Ruby Theatre in Chelan is said to be haunted by a former projectionist, but the ghost may be that of the old manager, Frank Potter (sometimes also spelled Petter, Patter and Porter, 1881–1919, thirty-eight years), who brutally murdered his wife and then committed suicide in 1919.

The Ruby Theatre was built in 1914 by its original owners, brothers Herbert R. and Morrison M. Kingman. It was named after Ruby Potter, the stepdaughter of its then manager, Frank Potter. Currently, the Ruby is the oldest continuously running movie theater in the state of Washington. The theater has a horseshoe balcony, a tin ceiling and a cast plaster proscenium arch. The Ruby is also considered one of the best-preserved movie theaters in the country.

In 1919, the theater was sold to a barber named Kelsey, a local from Chelan. He lived in a small apartment on the upper level behind the projector room. Frank Potter was employed by Kelsey, and for the most part, things seemed pretty normal.

Frank decided to leave the theater and began working on a ferry named the *Kittitas-Grant Counties* that traveled back and forth on the Columbia River. He worked hard and provided for his family. His mechanical skills were unmatched. But the history surrounding Mr. Frank Potter and his family is tragic.

The Ruby Theatre in Chelan is haunted by not only a former projectionist but also the old manager, Frank Potter, who committed a murder/suicide in 1919. *Courtesy of by Joe Mabel, 2008, via Wikimedia Commons.*

For all appearances, the Potter family was a loving and normal one. The couple had gotten married in 1909 and was eager to build a life together. For ten years, the family thrived, and all seemed well at the Potter residence in Vantage Ferry. Frank's wife, Carrie, and adopted daughter, Ruby, ran the Vantage Inn with great care, and Frank had established himself as an accomplished mechanic in town.

On June 15, 1919, the Potters happily went to a local photographer to have a family portrait taken together. But deep down, trouble was brewing. Somewhere along the line, in the next twenty-four hours, things would go terribly, terribly wrong.

On Sunday the sixteenth, at eleven o'clock at night, Frank snapped. Rumor had it he was insanely infatuated with his stepdaughter, Ruby. He snuck his wife a sleeping pill and then waited for her to fall asleep. After she passed out, he quietly crept upstairs to where Ruby was resting and rushed upon her— aggressively attacking her with criminal intent. Luckily, the fifteen-year-old was strong enough to be able to fight him off, and eventually, Frank gave up.

Frustrated and angry, he went back downstairs and approached his sleeping wife, Carrie B. Jane Foote (1878–1919, forty-one years), lay peacefully, unaware of the fate awaiting her within the next couple minutes.

Frank aimed his gun and ruthlessly shot her in the head, killing her instantly. Probably stunned by what he had just done, he quickly turned the revolver on his own skull and pulled the trigger.

Upstairs, Ruby heard the horrific sound of the revolver being fired—*twice*. She stayed in her bedroom, terrified, until about nine o'clock the next morning. When she thought all was safe, she slowly made her way down the stairs to the living room, where she witnessed the gruesome, bloody scene: her parents lying dead. Ruby quickly ran to her neighbor's house and later explained to authorities the dreadful murder-suicide that had occurred the night before.

Coroner Gregory held the inquest for the deceased couple.

No further details can be found about the aftermath of the event. Washington State Board of Health death certificate no. 95 reports that Frank committed suicide by "revolver to head." The 1910 census lists his wife's name as Karia (instead of the correct spelling, Carrie) and his stepdaughter as Ruby.

Nobody knows whose spirit is actually is haunting the theater. Is it the lovesick projectionist? Or is it possibly Frank Potter, who returned to a happier time in his life before the horrible tragedy?

NOTE: The Ruby Theatre is located at 135 East Woodin Avenue, Chelan, Washington 98816.

LAKE MONSTERS

As everyone knows, the most famous sea serpent of all time is the Loch Ness Monster. Also known as Nessie, this mythical creature is said to inhabit Loch Ness, a large freshwater lake near Inverness, Scotland. Loch Ness is located in the Scottish Highlands and has the largest volume of fresh water in Great Britain. Scholars have found references to "Nessie" in Scottish history dating to around AD 500.

But did you know there have been many, many more sightings of mysterious sea and lake monsters dating back hundreds of years? On September 25, 1808, the "Stronsay Sea Monster" was found in Scotland. This fascinating creature washed ashore on the island of Stronsay (formerly spelled Stronsa), in the Orkney Islands, after a massive storm. The gigantic creature was fifty-five feet long, with a fifteen-foot-long neck and a body circumference of about ten feet. It had three pairs of strange appendages—some believed they looked like wings. No one was ever able to formally identify the creature.

In 1907, Captain Sir A.H. Rostron of the ship *Carpathia* spotted an extremely long serpentlike creature just off the coast of Ireland. He claimed it stuck its eight-foot-long neck out of the water for all the crew to see.

In 1934, excited passengers and crew on the ship *Mauretania*, with the very credible Captain Reginald Peel at the wheel, spotted an unfamiliar creature at least sixty feet long with four large humps on its back about sixty miles east of Nassau, near the Bahamas.

Also in 1934, a twenty-five-foot-long sea creature washed ashore on a beach near Cherbourg, France, shocking locals and exciting reporters.

All around the world, the vast ocean hides a remarkable number of unknown species, so why couldn't our deepest lakes do the same? Did you know that strange water creatures have been reported in Eastern Washington?

LAKE CHELAN DRAGON

A two-hundred-year-old legend says that a mysterious monster lurks beneath the cold, murky waters of Lake Chelan. Lake Chelan is sixty miles long and can run 1,500 feet deep in places, making it the third-deepest lake in the United States as well as one of the largest and longest.

What makes Lake Chelan even more mysterious is that the very bottom of it has yet to be explored. What strange creature might be living down there?

The legend tells of a secret item that was snuck into a wooden chest and brought over in a ship from Fort Augustus in Scotland. In 1812, while the ship was sailing near the coast of Washington State, a violent storm erupted, causing chaos onboard. The captain fought to manage the course of the ship, while his crew struggled to stay aboard. In the commotion, the chest flew overboard and slowly sank down into the murky waters below.

It was believed the chest held a single precious egg from a mysterious creature. The story goes that when the chest went overboard, both the chest and the egg cracked open, releasing the secret hatchling into the ocean.

The local Entiat tribe knew about the puzzling lake creature. They called the body of water Tsi-Laan, or Deep Water, and they called the lake monster N'hah'hahat'q. Today, the creature is called the Dragon of Lake Chelan. This creature is said to have the legs and body of an alligator; the head and eyes of a serpent; sharp teeth; a long, scaly tail; and batlike wings—truly something from a horror movie. The N'hah'hahat'q is also believed to have supernatural powers.

Could the N'hah'hahat'q still be alive after over two hundred years? There are only a few species of fish that can live that long. The blackthroat rockfish (also called the rougheye rockfish) gets its name from the spines along its lower eyelid. These fish prefer to swim in deep waters, which makes them tough to spot. One rockfish caught off the Alaskan coast in 2013 was estimated to be more than two hundred years old! But a rockeye can typically only grow up to about forty inches—which would hardly qualify as the Lake Chelan monster.

The N'hah'hahat'q monster has been spotted by several locals over the years, but it is virtually impossible to capture.

In 1892, a strange water creature was seen by a young man playfully splashing around in the deep waters of Lake Chelan. Terrified, he frantically began swimming toward shore, but he was not quick enough. The creature grabbed ahold of him as his friends tried to pull him to the safety of the shore. The boys beat the monster with pieces of logs, trying to save their friend, but that did nothing to deter it. Tragically, it quickly pulled the boy back down into the water, never to be seen again. The survivors later described the beast as having the body of an alligator, the head and eyes of a snake, a scaly tail and batlike wings.

In 1910, three local men were fishing off a dock on Lake Chelan. Much to their surprise, they witnessed a gigantic creature swimming right in front of them. They told reporters that they thought the creature was about seventy-five feet long.

A two-hundred-plus-year-old legend about a mysterious monster that swims down deep below the surface of Lake Chelan persists. Local Native Americans called it N'hah'hahat'q. Here, a young boy prepares to row on Lake Chelan in 1907. *Courtesy of LOC #2018653421, Underwood & Underwood, Publishers, 1907.*

The "lake creatures" could also be sturgeon. Although not aggressive, sturgeons are among the largest fish, with some species growing to over eighteen feet. They are also among the longest-lived fishes, some living well over one hundred years. But that is still a far cry from the legendary seventy-five-foot-long, two-hundred-year-old monster.

Another possibility is the giant oarfish, a creature that has rarely been caught. As the name implies, these creatures are huge—they can grow up to fifty-six feet long and weigh six hundred pounds! But since the giant oarfish primarily inhabits saltwater environments, and Lake Chelan is freshwater, the oarfish can be ruled out.

Until the Dragon of Lake Chelan is caught, its identity will remain a mystery. The lake is known to have multiple underwater caverns—any of which a slippery monster could be hiding in.

THE ROCK LAKE TERROR

In Rock Lake, near the Idaho border in Eastern Washington, legend has it that a giant serpentlike creature named Rocky once ate an entire tribe of local Palouse Native Americans. The Nez Perce and other local tribes avoided Rock Lake due to this dangerous mythical creature. According to Indigenous beliefs, there exists a horned creature known as Mishipeshu that resides in deep lakes and rivers. Mishipeshu has the head and paws of a giant cat (often resembling a cougar or lynx), and its body is covered in hard scales. Along its back and tail, it sports strong, daggerlike spikes. In Indigenous mythology, underwater panthers like Mishipeshu are opposing yet complementary forces to the Thunderbirds, who are masters of the powers of the air. These formidable beings engage in eternal conflict.

Long ago, a Ho-Chunk Native fasted and prayed on the shores of Rock Lake until one of the water spirits, resembling a cat with a long tail and horns, rose from beneath the water. This creature magically granted him the promise of long life. The underwater panther remains a mysterious and powerful figure in Native American folklore, symbolizing both danger and protection.

Rock Lake is the deepest and largest of all scabland lakes left behind by the Missoula floods. These floods, which occurred about fifteen thousand years ago, scoured the landscape across Eastern Washington, forming a system of lakes called coulees. At its deepest, Rock Lake plunges to more than 360 feet, although the official measurement remains uncertain.

The story of the Rock Lake Monster was first told in 1867 by a man named Harbeck, who claimed to have seen a large lizard swimming in the lake. Harbeck even encountered it on land, hidden among reeds and vegetation along the shore. As he walked by, the creature raised its head, hissed at him and swiftly returned to the water. Other witnesses around the same time reported seeing a large, thick creature resembling a serpent swimming beneath the lake's surface.

In the late 1870s, a man named R. Hassman encountered the notorious beast. He mistook it for a large tree limb floating on the water but soon realized it was alive. Hassman attempted to stab it with his walking stick, and Rocky sprang to life, angrily thrashing about. Hassman couldn't hold off the monster any more than he could hold off an ox.

The most famous interaction with Rocky occurred in 1882. Two men, Ed McKenzie and D.W. Seybert, challenged each other to a rowboat race across the lake. As they rowed, they encountered Rocky. The creature was massive, and its presence was awe-inspiring. Whether they continued with the race or not, their encounter with the Rock Lake Terror became legendary.

In 1943, Rocky was seen for the last time. It is believed that the creature either died of old age or succumbed to some unknown mystery.

Was Rocky real? Opinions vary. Native American legends from the Ho-Chunk tribe in the Rock River area (near Rock Lake) still speak of a terrible monster, adding to the mystery surrounding this elusive creature.

SELMA LAKE MONSTER

Selma Lake, located in the Selkirk Mountains of Eastern Washington, has had its share of lake monster sightings. A picturesque alpine lake nestled within the rugged and scenic Selkirk Mountains, it lies in the Colville National Forest, which encompasses parts of northeastern Washington. The Selkirk mountain range spans the northern portion of the Idaho Panhandle, Eastern Washington and southeastern British Columbia and is part of a larger grouping of mountains, the Columbia Mountains. The majority of Selma Lake is relatively shallow, typically under ten feet deep. How can a large monster inhabit such shallow waters?

Yet multiple witnesses have claimed to have seen a bizarre creature—a long, serpentlike specimen—swimming in the lake's shallow waters. Nobody knows what the strange creature is or how long it has been prowling the lake.

In 1857, gold was discovered in the Selkirks. Coal, copper, marble, mercury, silver and zinc were also found in the mountains, which brought men clamoring for their share of the riches. This influx of people added to the number of reported Selma Lake monster sightings.

Many other mysterious lake monsters have been spotted throughout the United States. The fact that multiple witnesses have seen these creatures and that they have been seen in many locations brings more credibility to the stories of lake creatures located in Washington State. Some of the more fascinating sightings are:

ALKALI: A lake monster in Alkali Lake in Nebraska, said to be a forty-foot-long alligator-like creature with rough, grayish-brown skin and a hornlike appendage located between its eyes and nostrils.

ALTAMAHA-HA: In Altamaha River in Georgia, a thirty-foot-long creature with a snakelike head and flippers like a sea lion.

SOUTH BAY BESSIE: In Lake Erie in Ohio, snakelike and thirty to forty feet long, at least a foot in diameter, with a grayish color.

FLOSSIE: In Flathead Lake in Montana, a twenty- to forty-foot-long eel-like creature, brown to blue-black in color, with steel-black eyes.

MESHEKENABEK: In Lake Manitou in Indiana, a thirty-foot-long creature, dark in color, with a long neck with a horselike head.

SMETTY: In Lake De Smet in Wyoming. Has a head like a horse and a bony ridge down its back and is about forty feet long.

Can all these strange creatures simply be figments of people's overactive imaginations for hundreds of years? Probably not!

ALMIRA

Almira was first settled in the 1880s by Charles C. Davis (1830–1909, age seventy-eight), who purchased land and erected a small store to serve the few settlers in the area at the time. The Central Washington Railroad (later acquired by the Northern Pacific) was set to pass through the region by 1889. Land developers Odgers and Reed approached Davis to start a town on the site.

On seeing Davis's wife's name, Almira Ridgeway Davis, on the deed, the developers suggested christening the town under her name, thus giving birth to the town of Almira. (Prior to this, Davis's farm and post office had been called Davisine.)

With the railroad project assured, Almira was formally platted, and lots began to sell quickly. Contractors and businessmen erected temporary buildings for their stores. The railroad did indeed reach Almira in the fall of 1889, serving as the line's temporary terminus before being extended to Coulee City the following summer.

Despite the end of Almira as a rail terminal, it continued to thrive through 1890 with the establishment of a newspaper and the construction of many new buildings. In November 1890, Almira citizens voted for prohibition, temporarily making it the only dry town in the Big Bend Country. The town continued to experience growth, but the Panic of 1893 affected Almira, as it did many places across the country.

Later, in 1933, during construction of the Grand Coulee Dam, Almira was resurrected and served as the construction headquarters for the large Works Progress Administration (WPA) project. The town was dubbed the Gateway City to the Grand Coulee Dam.

ALMIRA HOTEL

In a town with a population under three hundred, a haunted hotel creates a bit of excitement! Witnesses have seen the apparitions of men in work clothes hanging out in the basement of the Almira Hotel. Room 21 is also reported to be haunted, although it is never used. Knocks, phantom footsteps and eerie voices mysteriously come from behind the locked door.

The first boardinghouse in Almira was opened in about 1885 by Charles C. Davis and his wife, Almira Ridgeway Davis. The first hotel built on the present site was the Northwestern Hotel, which Samuel Hyde bought in 1897 and renamed the Hotel Almira.

The new Almira Hotel was the third hotel to grace the town. Completed in 1918 at a cost of $60,000, it was a three-story building with approximately forty-five rooms. The ground floor housed commercial/retail bays, which hosted various eating and retail establishments over the years. The hotel also served as the home for the post office and the telephone office at different times.

In 1902, Frank Heffenish bought the Hotel Almira for $4,500, but his investment was short-lived. Just one year later, disaster struck when a fire originating in the kitchen destroyed the hotel and surrounding buildings.

In 1905, Boone Thompson and Willis Schrock rebuilt the hotel on the corner of Third and Main Streets for $14,000.

Yet another tragic fire commenced on December 8, 1916, which caused major damage. It started when the combustion of paint and oil ignited flames in the basement. The fire was not discovered until 5:15 a.m. the following morning, but by then, the blaze was uncontrollable. The Thompson & Schrock building, which housed the Hotel Almira, the Union Supply Store, R.L. Drinkard Clothing and the Pastime Billiard Parlor, were also lost to the fire—an estimated loss of $70,000–$90,000.

Again, the hotel was rebuilt, to the tune of $60,000. The three-story brick hotel was re-erected even bigger and better and would now offer forty-five comfortable rooms and a nice café. It also housed the new post office and telephone office.

In 1922, the hotel got a remodel and some updates, and during the 1920s, the hotel prospered.

In 1934, the proprietor was George McDonald. He prided himself on the hotel and taking care of its guests. But soon, the Great Depression caused financial strain.

Lack of help caused the hotel to shut its doors for a brief period during 1942, when J.H. MacDonald was the owner. World War II caused a lot of stress for many families and businesses. By then, the hotel had been continuously running for forty years. After the war ended in 1945, when work on the dam resumed, most laborers moved closer to the project to newer, bigger cities like Grand Coulee and Coulee City.

In 1960, Highway 2 was diverted to bypass Almira, causing more strain on the local businesses. The hotel portion stayed closed for a while, but the new cocktail lounge, called the Wheat Room, catered to locals for the next forty years. In 2006, the hotel was added to the National Register of Historic Places.

No one knows who is haunting their old stomping ground at the Almira Hotel, but it is believed they loved the hotel so much when they were alive that they are simply refusing to leave.

NOTE: Almira Hotel is located at 3 North Third Street, Almira, Washington 99103.

GRAND COULEE DAM

People claim that the spirits of the workers who died while working on the Grand Coulee Dam project haunt the enormous structure. Strange orbs of light and gray shadows have been spotted over the crashing water above the dam. Are these actual spirits or simply reflections from the lights and water?

During the construction of the dam, many folks and workers stayed at the Almira Hotel while looking for more permanent living situations. A shuttle would haul the workers back and forth from the hotel to the job site. The Grand Coulee Dam project caused the tiny town to explode. Over 350 families moved to Almira after securing employment at the project. It took 11,000 men and 27 million hours of labor to divert the river, execute the foundation and pour and place the incredible 12 million cubic yards of concrete. When completed, the dam stood 550 feet tall and 500 feet wide.

Although the dam brought progress to the area, it also created a more sinister side. A recorded seventy-seven men were killed due to the harsh working conditions and many fatal falls occurred on the project between 1933 and 1941. Tragically, four more people died during construction of the Third Powerhouse (1967–1975) bringing the total to eighty-one. (The Third Powerhouse was a crucial upgrade that enhanced the Grand Coulee Dam's ability to provide clean energy and made it the largest power station in the United States by nameplate capacity, boasting 6,809 megawatts of power.)

A seven-ton shaft monument was commissioned to be erected in honor of these men, but failure to secure payment halted its installation.

For more information on the proposed monument and a complete list of the men who died while constructing the Grand Coulee Dam, please visit https://www.newgs.org/cpage.php?pt=81.

Some interesting facts about the Grand Coulee Dam:

The dam can produce a total of 6,809 megawatts from 33 hydroelectric generators. That is more than three times the generating capacity of the Hoover Dam (which generates only 2,080 megawatts).

The dam is one of the largest concrete structures in the world, standing 550 feet high and measuring 5,223 feet long.

The Grand Coulee took eight years to build, employing thousands of men during the Great Depression.

As workers excavated, exposing the bedrock foundation for the dam, others drilled test holes from 30 to a whopping 200 feet deep.

More than 2,000 miles of one-inch cooling pipes were carefully embedded in the walls of the dam to carry away the massive heat generated during the concrete curing process and prevent dangerous cracking.

At times, crews worked nonstop for 24 hours, placing an average of one cubic yard (202 gallons) of concrete every four seconds!

In 1942, there was an enormous demand for the electrical power necessary to make aluminum, which was essential for World War II production of planes and ships. It was the Grand Coulee that powered the production of plutonium at the nearby Hanford Site, which figured prominently in the making of the atomic bomb.

Grand Coulee Dam after completion in 1942. Tragically, seventy-seven men lost their lives while building the ginormous dam, and they now haunt it. *Courtesy of LOC #2007663008, Charles A. Libby & Son, photographer.*

Almost one hundred men died during construction of the Grand Coulee Dam. Safety conditions were terrifying, and men's lives were at risk daily. *Courtesy of LOC #2008676664, U.S. Bureau of Reclamation.*

Above: Grand Coulee Dam in 1937, during construction. Four more people died during construction of the Third Powerhouse (1967–75), bringing the total number of deaths to eighty-one. *Courtesy of LOC #2008677050, Bureau of Reclamation, U.S. Department of the Interior.*

Right: Four unidentified men perch precariously in and on a large casing section. Eleven thousand men risked their lives every day during Grand Coulee Dam's eight years of construction. *Courtesy of LOC #2008676662, U.S. Bureau of Reclamation.*

There is no way of knowing which of the eighty-one deceased men might be haunting the dam, and the strange lights hovering over the water and eerie orbs moving mysteriously about offer no clues. The unusual paranormal activity associated with the Grand Coulee Dam will possibly continue forever.

UFOs OVER GRAND COULEE DAM

Many people have witnessed strange and unexplained aircraft hovering over the massive dam. Since day one of its construction in 1933, credible witnesses, workers and tourists have logged dozens of reports of unidentified flying objects. Only a few of the eleven thousand workers were brave enough to come forward and say what they saw. During an era when work was hard to find, many felt it was not worth losing their job over incidents they could not explain. So they kept their mouths shut and their jobs secure.

One family that was camping nearby reported being abducted by a large, dark aircraft that was so massive it blocked out the starry sky. The campers felt enveloped in warm air and then found themselves somehow transported up into the spaceship. Although they returned unharmed, the frightening memory haunted them for the rest of their lives.

Was the family actually abducted, or was it some sort of bizarre group hallucination?

LATAH CREEK AND THE GHOSTS OF THE PALOUSE

The story of the Ghosts of Hangman Creek (now known as Latah Creek) dates to 1858, when seventeen Palouse Indians were hanged beside the creek by the cruel orders of Colonel George Wright (1803–1865, age sixty-two). The identities of those hanged remains a mystery, and Wright's reasons for doing so was possibly to make a statement or show his strength in the situation, as he also ordered over one thousand of the Palouse's horses to be cruelly slaughtered.

During this tragic time, extreme tensions were brewing between the American immigrants who were encroaching on tribal land and the local

John Owens was hanged for his heinous crimes near Latah Creek (pictured here), and his ghost is said to roam the riverbanks. *Courtesy of U.S. National Oceanic and Atmospheric Administration.*

Native Americans. During the 1850s, tensions escalated even more as territorial authorities forced tribes to sign treaties relinquishing much of their ancestral territory. Many Indigenous people bitterly resented these treaties.

Following the tragic events in 1858 when seventeen Native Americans were hanged, the Palouse tribe faced significant challenges and upheaval.

The trauma of witnessing the executions and the loss of their leaders had a profound impact on Palouse culture and beliefs. Despite the loss of their leaders and the despicable trauma inflicted on them, the Palouse people continued to resist colonization by White settlers and fight for their rights.

But the Palouse continued to face massive ongoing pressure from territorial authorities and military forces for years to come. Their spirits broken, many Palouse reluctantly adapted to the changing circumstances by slowly integrating into White settler communities, seeking employment or participating in trade with the Americans.

But unnecessary violence and new diseases took a toll on the Palouse population. Many Palouse died due to the conditions they feared and faced the most.

Hangman's Creek is now haunted by the seventeen Palouse who were tragically killed, their angry spirits wanting revenge for their deaths and the breakdown of their culture. Many of the dead involved were never personally listed in historical records, but instead were buried in a mass grave, their names unknown for all eternity.

NOTE: Colonel George Wright and his wife, Margaret Wallace Forster Wright (1806–1865, age fifty-nine), were lost at sea and died in the wreck of the steamer *Brother Jonathan* at Point St. George, Crescent City, California, on July 30, 1865. The ill-fated *Brother Jonathan*, a paddle steamer, struck an uncharted rock near Point St. George. The ship was carrying 244 passengers and crew, along with a large shipment of gold. Tragically, only 19 people survived, making it the deadliest shipwreck up to that time on the Pacific Coast of the United States. Based on the passenger and crew list, it is believed that 225 people lost their lives in this maritime disaster. The bodies of Colonel Wright and his wife were recovered in California's Shelter Cove, 150 miles from the wreck. Remarkably, the ship's location remained unknown until 1993, and a portion of the gold was eventually recovered in 1996 when a mini submarine detected a "glint" on the ocean floor near the wreckage site. Divers subsequently found gold coins, and during future expeditions, they recovered a total of 1,207 gold coins, primarily $20 double eagles, in near-mint condition. Many coins still lie below the sand, hidden from eager divers.

Spokane

The prehistoric area now called the city of Spokane was once home to many hunter-gatherer communities who lived off the abundant fish and game native to the lands. Scientists have discovered early human remains that date to eight thousand to thirteen thousand years ago.

The name Spokane is derived from the Spokane tribe, meaning either Children of the Sun or Sun People in the Salish language.

The Spokane Falls area (the *e* was added to Spokan in 1883, and "Falls" was dropped in 1891) faced many difficulties during the Great Fire of 1889, when many of its wooden structures burned to the ground. The fire ravaged more than thirty blocks of the city's commercial area, and property losses were immense. Remarkably, only one person lost his life: George Davis. Nervously seeking refuge from the flames, Davis jumped from his second-story room at the Arlington Hotel. His injuries proved fatal, and he later died at Sacred Heart Hospital.

As tragic as the fire was, no time was wasted in rebuilding the beloved city by its business owners and city officials. The unfortunate fire set the stage for an exciting building boom as the city rose from the gray ashes and promoted significant changes in the city's infrastructure. Nearly twenty thousand citizens rebounded from their shock and quickly got to work replacing fire-susceptible wooden buildings with permanent stone and brick structures. Architects like Chauncey B. Seaton played a pivotal role in designing the new buildings that would define Spokane's future. A new carriage and wagon shop, the New York Brewery, a saloon, plumbing services, a cigar shop, a wine store and a liquor store—all continued to thrive during the construction. To ensure future safety, the city strictly prohibited any new wooden structures in or near the newly rising brick buildings downtown, and an electric fire alarm system was installed to enhance protection. Even better, Spokane eagerly established a professional, paid fire department equipped with new horse-drawn equipment.

Many of these brick buildings still grace Spokane's streets today. One local favorite is the Bodie Block/1889 Building located at 427 West Main Avenue. This three-story brick building is the oldest remaining structure from the post-fire era. It exemplifies the city's exuberant rebirth after the disaster, and it features Romanesque Revival elements, including prominent semicircular arches and richly detailed brick and stone-face granite trim (a decorative but protective border around the edges that prevents chipping or damage, while also adding an elegant touch to the overall design).

Another Spokane icon is the Fernwell Building, designed by architect Kirtland Cutter, a historic office building downtown. The Bennett Block is an enduring brick structure, along with the Review Building and the old Coeur d'Alene Hotel building.

If the walls and floors of these notable historic buildings could talk, they would tell tales of hardships, successes, tragedies—and even love stories. Some believe ghostly spirits still keep watch over their buildings, forever eager to serve the next customer or make their presence known.

THE UNSOLVED MURDER OF TRIXIE

The sad ghost of a local woman named Trixie still wanders the area of old Heller Block (located on Howard Street between Riverside Avenue and Main Street) in Spokane. This woman who answered to many names was madly in love with her husband—but the lovesick lady's life did not end well. Sometimes she went by Mrs. Mamie Fredericks, other times Mrs. Layton and sometimes, if the mood struck her—simply Trixie.

She was fatefully head over heels in love with her husband, Albert Layton—but he was a known womanizer, gambler and notorious drunk. Trixie would often complain about his extramarital affairs, and later she would tire and take her own lover, a married man living in Butte, Montana, known only as Fred.

On that fateful evening in 1892, Mr. Layton and Trixie were in apartment no. 12 in the boardinghouse on Heller Block, enjoying the warmth of a fire. They had been drinking, and both were fairly intoxicated, so Mr. Layton lay down on the sofa and quickly fell asleep.

At about ten o'clock, Trixie was struggling to stoke the fire and Mrs. Belle Anderson, her landlady, came in to help her. Belle noticed Trixie was crying. When Belle asked why she was upset, Trixie told her, "Mr. Layton has a desire for other women. I cannot live without him and would rather kill myself than have him live with another woman!" Belle noticed the room was in disarray: clothes were tossed everywhere, and the bed was a mess, all of which made her uncomfortable. She helped Trixie with the fire, then hurriedly left the apartment.

Sometime after ten, Belle noticed that everything seemed to be settled down, and people in the complex were finally going to bed for the night. Later that night, around 1:15 a.m., Patrol Officer Peter Nimes heard loud cries coming from under the nearby Howard Street Bridge. He ran to see what was happening and discovered a lone man frantically splashing in the water below. Officer Nimes and Inspector Gough carefully made their way down the bank and found Layton sitting casually on a small raft floating in the Spokane River.

The man was completely covered in blood!

He was apparently intoxicated and singing obscene songs at the top of his lungs. Nimes quickly pulled the stranger from the river and hauled him to the station. Officers G.G. Webb and O.F. Asmussen quickly recognized the drunk as Al (Allen) Layton. They said that the Laytons had moved to Spokane from San Francisco just a few months prior and that Al had been dealing faro at the Richelieu Gambling Room in town to make ends meet.

Webb and Asmussen offered to go to Layton's apartment and advise his wife to come retrieve her husband and take him home to sleep the whiskey off. It seems odd that the officers did not take his blood-soaked clothes seriously.

When the officers arrived at room no. 12 in the boardinghouse on Heller Block, they opened the door to a ghastly scene. Mrs. Layton (Trixie) was dead, her head half blown off, lying in a thick pool of her own blood. On searching the crime scene, they found dozens of unsent love letters to a man named Fred and also letters from Trixie to her family. A blood-soaked Smith & Wesson lay on top of a bureau. Captain Coverly and Coroner Weems were quickly summoned to the gory scene. They also found a pencil and a handwritten note that read:

> *I love you Al. I am to blame for all of it. Al, forgive me, my darling.*
> *— Trix*

Was this a suicide note or just a letter of apology? Did Trixie really write the letter herself, or was it some kind of cover-up? Was Trixie blaming herself for her husband's extramarital affairs or for finally having one herself? Did Al find the hidden love letters to Fred and become furious enough to kill her? Was Fred real or simply a ploy to make her husband jealous?

Captain Coverly took a closer look at the victim. The bullet had entered her right temple and exited the left, working its way completely through her brain. She was wearing a black dress and a fur coat at the time of her demise.

The Andersons, landlords of the Heller Block, told the police that the Laytons had been quarreling for days and they had recently been forced to give the Laytons an eviction notice. They also demanded the Laytons pay for their two weeks' worth of back rent.

Oddly, when the officers questioned other tenants in the building, no one claimed to have heard the gunshot that tragically took Trixie's life. How could that be?

The officers determined that a struggle had definitely taken place inside the room, and all the evidence led to the cold-blooded murder of twenty-seven-year-old Trixie. Back at the station, the forty-five-year-old, blood-soaked Mr. Layton would now have to talk.

After a few hours, when Layton was more levelheaded and the booze was wearing off, the interrogation began. Layton slowly began telling Inspector Gough about the events of the previous fatal night.

From actual testimony transcribed in the courtroom during the inquest: "I was in my room lying down and had fallen asleep. When I awoke, Trixie was in her cloak and was preparing to leave. She said she was going to Kitty Miller's. I said to her, 'If I were you, I would blow my brains out before I would go there.' She at once replied, 'Well, then I will do it,' and pulled out a gun then shot herself in the head!"

Layton claimed that after she shot herself, Trixie sat down in a chair. Then she got up and tried to get onto the bed but fell down at the head of it.

I tried to get her up on the bed but was not strong enough, and after two or three tries I gave it up. I realized that she was dead and all hope in life was gone for me. I took my hat and walked out into the street and down to the river as fast as I could and jumped in, intending to drown myself. I did not speak to anyone on my way to the river. I loved the woman dearly and am satisfied that just one kind word from me would have saved her life. I do not know whether I touched the gun after the shooting or not. In fact, I was crazy drunk and did not really know what was done or what I did.

The man's testimony would seem valid enough to call Layton's guilt into question, but the jury, for some reason, could not reach a conclusion as to whether or not he was actually guilty of murder. They requested to wait until the autopsy was finalized before making their decision.

Doctor Doolittle eagerly conducted the autopsy. Trixie's skull was fractured from ear to ear. The bullet was extracted and determined to have come from a .32 caliber gun. The wound was profound at the right temple, and it was apparent that the shot was taken at point-blank range. There were heavy gunpowder stains under the skin but none on the surface of the skin. Trixie's forefinger had evidence of black powder on it.

Layton would remain in jail until the verdict was determined.

Strangely, after deliberating, the jury decided there was not enough evidence to convict Layton of murder, and he was acquitted.

So did Trixie really commit suicide?

After the trial ended, a saloonkeeper from San Francisco, California, disclosed that Trixie was actually Mrs. May Fredrickson, a member of the elite 400s Club—a private club reserved for only four hundred of the richest and most influential citizens in a given city. He thought she had possibly gotten a divorce from her husband in San Francisco and believed she also had four children living somewhere in Oakland, California. Was Trixie really a member of the 400s Club?

No more records can be found about this mysterious incident—and no real answer about whether Trixie's death was a tragic suicide or a murder at the hands of her drunken husband.

Perhaps her horrible death, regardless of how she died, causes her restless spirit to wander the area of Heller Block in Spokane to this day—searching for her husband for all eternity. Or is she seeking revenge from beyond the grave for her ghastly death?

DAVENPORT HOTEL

Some question who really haunts the exquisite and beautiful Davenport Hotel in downtown Spokane. But who *wouldn't* want to roam its elegant rooms for all eternity?

The Davenport Hotel stands out as one of the most historically luxurious and elegant buildings to be found anywhere. Wandering from room to room and from floor to floor, one is completely enveloped in some of the most impressive architectural details ever imagined.

The hotel is so artistically divine and extravagant it is almost hard to comprehend. Every nook and cranny has some sort of phenomenal detail to explore and ponder. The lobby's soaring ceilings, intricate moldings and art glass panels create an atrium effect, making it a truly breathtaking space to enter.

The building underwent expansions in both 1917 and 1929. The Davenport Hotel was added to the National Register of Historic Places in 1975. The Davenport Hotel thrived for decades, hosting celebrities, politicians and tourists seeking only the finest in luxury.

But sadly, after changing hands multiple times, the hotel fell into disrepair. In the mid-twentieth century, changing travel patterns and economic challenges had contributed to its decline. The hotel faced severe financial difficulties, and the maintenance of the massive building became a huge struggle.

Eventually, in 1985, the Davenport Hotel closed its doors to the public, falling into serious adverse conditions and even facing the threat of demolition. Louis Davenport Jr., the son of the hotel's founder, was hesitant to buy the deteriorating property as it was so overwhelming. The immense scale of restoration needed was daunting, and the financial burden weighed heavily.

Thankfully, in 2002, two visionary developers, Walt and Karen Worthy, restored it in a $38 million renovation preserving its historic charm and restoring the building to its former glory. Louis Davenport Jr.'s decision to sell the family hotel allowed the Davenport to thrive, soon becoming again a cherished landmark in Spokane.

The Worthys sold the hotel in 2021 to a private equity firm, and today, Marriot holds the property.

The Davenport Hotel has its share of intriguing stories, including one about a tragic incident involving Ellen McNamara, a wealthy widow visiting from New York. In 1920, she met her chilling fate when she oddly stepped onto the glass ceiling while strolling along the catwalk with a friend. The glass shattered, and she plummeted down, crashing onto the dining room floor to her death. Her spirit is said to linger within the hotel, making it one of the most haunted hotels in Washington State. Guests and staff have reported strange occurrences, including unexplained noises, cold spots and eerie sensations. Some believe that Ellen's restless soul continues to wander the halls, forever tied to the place of her tragic fall. Paranormal investigators have even recorded the voice of a dead woman asking, "Where did I go?"

Some believe another woman's spirit haunts the Davenport. While living, she apparently loved the hotel very much. Her ghost has been spotted by several guests and night shift employees. She is described as an apparition walking the halls wearing a bathrobe and slippers, peering curiously over the balcony. Some believe she is a protective presence, perhaps even watching over the guests who are staying at the grand hotel. She is believed to have met her end within its historic walls. Her presence, shrouded in mystery, continues to intrigue guests and staff alike and her spirit roams the mezzanine and tends to pop in unexpectedly. Whether she was a former guest, a long-serving employee or a spirit drawn to the hotel's grandeur, her story remains a haunting enigma within the Davenport's opulent corridors.

One of many exquisite architectural details in the Davenport Hotel. Countless mysterious patterns, figurines, symbols and reliefs adorn its walls and ceilings. *Courtesy of author.*

Another female apparition is seen walking around the upper story above the fabulous dining area. It is possibly the ghost of a former admirer of the hotel. Marie Antoinette "Nettie" Fowler McCormick (1835–1923, age eighty-eight) was a prominent philanthropist and one of the wealthiest women in the late nineteenth and early twentieth centuries. She donated to various worthy causes in Spokane and was well known for her fabulous generosity. She was born in Brownsville, New York, and married Cyrus Hall McCormick, the eldest son of inventor Robert McCormick, in 1858. Together, they had seven children and became fabulously wealthy.

It is said that Nettie's beautiful ghost haunts the Davenport Hotel, which she helped fund. She was a frequent and welcome guest at the Davenport during her lifetime. She died on July 5, 1923, at her home in Lake Forest, Illinois, but her heart remained at the Davenport.

Guests and staff have reported encountering Nettie's ghostly presence many times in the hotel. Perhaps the elegant and lavish Marie Antoinette ballroom at the Davenport was designed especially for Nettie? No expense was spared during construction: its three original chandeliers were purchased for an unbelievable $10,000 each in 1914. Today, the exquisite ballroom can be rented out for special events and weddings. Maybe Nettie hangs around to experience the lovely celebrations?

Others think the Davenport is haunted by its founder, Mr. Louis Davenport himself! Davenport used to check on his guests in the early hours of the morning, carefully roaming the halls of the massive hotel, making sure everything was in perfect condition. Perhaps now his ghost refuses to stop working and is forever managing his glorious hotel.

Llewellyn "Louis" Marks Davenport (1868–1951, age eighty-three) was a fascinating local legend in early Spokane, an incredible businessman and an inspiration to many. Working tirelessly, Louis moved his way up from selling waffles out of a tent to eventually overseeing the grandest hotel in all of Washington. Louis was born in Pawnee City, Nebraska, on July 14, 1868. His family moved to Red Bluff, California, in 1880 when he was just twelve years old. At the age of twenty, he arrived in Spokane with only a few dollars to his name to work during the summer in his uncle's restaurant, the Pride of Spokane.

After the Great Spokane Fire of August 1889, Louis (just twenty-one at the time) started his own business called Davenport's Waffle Foundry, reportedly armed with only two tents, a few bucks and some salvaged furniture. Soon, his establishment was bustling. He eventually turned his establishment into one of the busiest restaurants in the Northwest.

The ghost of Ellen McNamara, who tragically fell through the glass ceiling of the lobby (pictured here), still haunts the dining room of the Davenport Hotel. *Postcard courtesy of SPL #5416, 1915-1920.*

His unannounced courtship of and subsequent marriage to Verus Smith (1878–1967, age eighty-nine) took the city by surprise. They married at three o'clock in the afternoon at the St. Thomas Episcopal Church in New York City on August 30, 1906. Prior to their marriage, Verus had been attending school in Portland, Oregon. Little is known about Verus, and she remains a bit of a Spokane mystery. We know she was born in 1878 in Oakland, Oregon, and her parents were John Smith (from Missouri) and Martha Evans (from Tennessee). We also know she lovingly supported her husband, Louis, right up until his death.

Spokane continued to expand, and the city's population grew. The year the Davenports got married, a group of Spokane businessmen envisioned a grand hotel to accommodate the booming area's travelers. They eagerly approached Louis Davenport (now age thirty-eight) to build and oversee this extremely ambitious project, as they knew he was the man to get the job done. Louis enlisted the aid of famed local architect Kirtland Cutter (1860–1939, age seventy-nine) to design the hotel adjoining his current restaurant. Over the next few years, many celebrities traveled to Spokane and dined at Davenport's, including President William Howard Taft. Forever striving to improve things, Davenport slowly added onto the restaurant and hotel with more dining rooms, a larger kitchen and even more ballrooms.

After much challenging work, the 406-room Davenport Hotel finally opened in August 1914. It cost about $2 million (almost $60 million in today's dollars) to construct. With its Spanish Renaissance–style main lobby, Isabella Dining Hall, Italian Gardens restaurant, Marie Antoinette Ballroom and fabulously ornate Hall of Doges, it quickly became known as the grandest hotel in America.

In 1915, when he was asked about the decorative symbols used in the hotel, Louis Davenport said,

> *In the old Spanish homes, it was the custom to display medallions carrying the portraits of honored ancestors and distinguished members of the family. This accounts for their frequent appearance throughout the lobby. Prominent in the ornamentation is the griffin. This, as used here, has the body of a lion, symbolic of strength, and the wings and head of an eagle, emblematic of alertness, swiftness, and rapidity of execution. The dolphin, which figures in the ornamentation, is always associated with mythology and sociability.*

Louis Davenport was meticulous about his hotel. His establishment was known for its excellent service and exquisite elegance, offered at reasonable rates. He worked tirelessly on the creation and management of the hotel most of his life.

In 1907, Louis and his wife, Verus E., had a son named Louis Jr. (1907–1987, age eighty). The family lived happily in room no. 1128 in the hotel most of their lives.

Mr. Davenport and his family also owned a 440-acre summer estate they named Flower Field, located on the Little Spokane River, in Nine Mile Falls, Washington. (Later, the St. George's Preparatory School was built on the Flower Field estate, intertwining a legacy of learning with the land's natural beauty.)

After decades of demanding work, in 1928, Mr. Davenport was able to buy out all the shareholders and proudly became the sole owner of the Davenport Hotel.

The Davenports enjoyed a few hard-earned vacations, and in 1921, they visited Honolulu, Hawaii. In July 1923, they sailed on the RMS *Aquitania* out from New York City to explore Cherbourg, France.

Louis eventually retired and sold his establishment on April 26, 1945, to the William Edris Company of Seattle, for $1.5 million, but he and his wife, Verus, continued to live in room no. 1128 as part of the deal. He died in 1951 on the eleventh floor; Washington State Death Certificate No.13352 stated

The incredibly ornate Hall of Doges in the Davenport Hotel lures both tourists and mischievous spirits with its magnificent beauty. *Courtesy of author.*

The fantastic stained-glass ceiling in the Davenport's Peacock Lounge is a masterpiece, created in 2022 by Spokane artist Susan Kim, using more than five thousand pieces of glass. *Courtesy of author.*

that the cause was heart disease. Verus continued to live in their apartment at the Davenport until her death in 1967 at age eighty-nine from cerebral thrombosis. The Davenport spirit lives on forever within the elegant walls of their beautiful hotel.

Louis Davenport was very particular about his hotel and worked tirelessly to keep everything perfect. Late at night, Mr. Davenport's spirit still roams the halls of his hotel, continuously looking over the place, making sure everything is still in tip-top shape.

The premier Governor Suite on the penthouse floor spans an impressive 2,360 square feet, and the hotel has catered to many famous people over the years. Other ghosts that might pop into the Davenport Hotel (since they loved staying there every time they visited Spokane) could be Bing Crosby, Bob Hope, Amelia Earhart, Clark Gable, Charles Lindbergh, Betty White, Johnny Cash, Nat King Cole, Queen Marie of Romania, Liberace, Babe Ruth, Rock Hudson and many more. The rock band Fleetwood Mac also loved to stay at the Davenport Hotel when entertaining in Spokane.

Keep your eyes and ears open as you explore this beautiful building, and hopefully you will see a ghost peering around the corner!

NOTE: The Historic Davenport Hotel is located at 10 South Post Street, Spokane, Washington. It operates under the name the Historic Davenport Hotel within the Davenport Hotel Collection brand, affiliated with Marriott's Autograph Collection Hotels. Call (509) 789-6808 or (509) 455-8888 or visit https://www.marriott.com.

MONTVALE HOTEL

The ghost of Louis Davenport is also reportedly seen at the Montvale Hotel. The historic building is nestled in Spokane's arts and entertainment district and has a captivating history that intertwines elegance with whispers of the supernatural.

Louis was the hotel's founder, and it is said he loves to wander around Montvale's corridors, casually clad in his bathrobe and slippers, as if still overseeing the legacy he built. Guests have reported mysterious occurrences: bellhops in 1920s uniforms who vanish into thin air, accompanied by phantom cigar smokers. The scent of cigars commonly lingers, though no visible source exists.

Originally built in 1889 by Judge John W. Binkley (1856–1931, age seventy-five) the three-story redbrick building was named after Montvale Farms, his country estate on the Little Spokane River. Binkley served as a probate judge for Spokane County in 1885 and 1886.

The Montvale offered commercial space on the ground floor, with thirty rooms on each of the two upper floors. The Montvale had both men's and women's bathrooms, considered a luxury at the time—each hosting two toilets and one bathtub. Room rates were typically one to two dollars per week, or five dollars a month! As a single-room occupancy (SRO) hotel, the

Montvale served Spokane in various roles over the years. It functioned as an apartment building and a brothel and was even used as an emergency ammunition supply room during World War II.

After Binkley's death, his daughter sold the building to his close friend and tenant William Kilmer of Kilmer Hardware. The hardware store located in the building was open from 1913 until the sale of the building in 1966, when Sam A. Postell purchased the Montvale for $125,000.

During the Expo '74 (officially known as the International Exposition on the Environment, Spokane 1974, the event was a world's fair held from May 4 to November 3, 1974, in downtown Spokane) it was used as a youth hostel, but after Expo was over, the hotel was abandoned for thirty years.

Luckily, in January 2005, the Montvale Hotel underwent a remarkable transformation. It was restored and reopened as a thirty-six-room boutique hotel. With the demolition of the Pennington Wing at the Davenport Hotel, the Montvale gained the distinction of being Spokane's oldest hotel. Today, it stands as one of Spokane's premier hotels, alongside the Davenport Hotel and the Hotel Lusso. Today, the remarkable building is available for special events as well.

It would be great fun to bump into the ghost of Louis Davenport while staying at the Montvale!

NOTE: If you seek a thrill, consider joining the real-life ghost tours that start at the Montvale Hotel. As darkness descends, explore its haunted corners, perhaps catching a glimpse of the spectral residents. The tour concludes at the Sapphire Lounge, where spirits—both liquid and ethereal—await. The Montvale Hotel is at 1005 West First Avenue, Spokane, Washington. Call (509) 624–1518 or visit https://montvalespokane.com. Please check to see if the tours are still available.

CAMPBELL MANSION

The Campbell House is a historic mansion hosting 13,700 square foot of space, designed by the famous architect Kirtland Cutter in 1898. The glorious estate was built for Amasa Basaliel Campbell (1845–1912, age sixty-seven); his beautiful wife, Grace (1859–1924, age sixty-five); and their only daughter, Helen (1892–1964, age seventy-two). Campbell married Grace Fox on March 26, 1890, in Youngstown, Ohio. He made a fortune in mining exploration and various other operations in the Coeur d'Alene mining region

Grace Campbell's exquisite reception room, where the ghost of the lovely lady of the house still roams. *Courtesy of LNTiedt, 2019, via Wikimedia.*

northeast of Spokane. His first beautiful Victorian mansion is located in Wallace, Idaho, on Cedar Street, where the family lived from 1890 to 1898; it still stands as a testament to Campbell's wealth. The family continued to live in Wallace while their Spokane estate was being constructed.

Campbell always partnered with longtime friend and colleague John Finch (1852–1925, age seventy-three) on business matters. Amasa Campbell, Patsy Clark and John Finch founded Hecla Mining Company in the state of Idaho on October 14, 1891. Over the years, Hecla became a leading domestic producer of silver and lead. Campbell and Finch were also successful in founding the Standard and Mammoth Mines near Wallace, Idaho. These mines became so successful that by 1903, they had sold them for $3 million

The Campbell Mansion is now the Northwest Museum of Arts and Culture, and visitors see the ghost of Grace floating around the rooms. *Courtesy of Washington State Archives (hereafter WSA).*

(approximately $104,572,500 in today's money!) to a joint venture backed by the Rockefeller and Gould families. The two later became neighbors when Finch also built a beautiful Spokane mansion just two houses to the west of Campbell's estate.

The Campbell mansion is one of the most popular tourist destinations in the Pacific Northwest. For one, it is known for being a unique piece of late nineteenth-century architecture. The Campbell House is now part of the Northwest Museum of Arts and Culture. Some visitors claim to have seen the beautiful ghost of Grace floating in and out of the rooms. Others believe the portrait of Mr. Campbell that hangs in the mansion has magic powers and he can still keep watch over his home—his eyes seem to follow you as you tour his mansion! Other visitors claim to hear the sounds of small children laughing and running through the rooms—when there are no children present! Could one of these childlike apparitions be Helen's spirit?

For the last six months of his life, Campbell was unable to speak, and for a month, he was unable to eat; nourishment was injected through a silver tube into his throat. Desperate, he consulted the Mayo brothers at Rochester, Minnesota, and other cancer specialists in New York, but nothing could be done to save his life. He died on February 16, 1912, in Spokane, Washington, due to the cancerous growth on his neck. He is buried in Greenwood Memorial Terrace in Spokane with his lovely wife, Grace, to his right and his brother Isaac Newton (1858–1903, age forty-five) to his left.

A tragic rumor persists that while the Campbells were living in Spokane, a brutal assailant broke into their home, murdered three of their four children and kidnapped the fourth child, who was never returned or found. This horrible legend has no factual basis, as the Campbells only had one child, Helen, who married William Weaver Powell on June 27, 1917, in Spokane, where they made their home. The Powells had three children during their marriage: William (1918–1982), Allen (1920–1944) and John (1925–2012). Allan Campbell Powell sadly died on January 5, 1944, when he was just twenty-three years old. A second lieutenant in the U.S. Army, he was killed in action on January 5, 1944, in Rhone, Draguignan, France.

Helen died peacefully in Spokane, Washington, with her friends and family at her side.

Perhaps the beautiful mansion is haunted by the Campbell family because the estate is so amazing—who would want to leave it? Some say Grace's exquisite figure can be seen casually walking down the stairs toward the home's main entrance. Is she still seeking visitors to lavishly entertain as she so elegantly did when she was alive? It was said that to be invited to one of the dinner parties at the Campbell mansion was quite an honor.

Grace died in 1924, and her casket was positioned temporarily in the drawing room of their mansion, surrounded by dozens of pink roses and lavender chrysanthemums. Over 250 attended her funeral, as Grace was so well loved and admired by so many Spokane citizens.

Note: The Campbell mansion is located at 2316 West First Avenue, S pokane, Washington, 99201. Please visit https://www.northwestmuseum.org for more information.

PATSY CLARK MANSION

I am willing to take a fling at anything there is money in.
—*Patsy Clark, 1905*

Another one of Spokane's most astonishing mansions is the personal estate of mining millionaire Patrick "Patsy" Clark (1851–1915, age sixty-four) who was born in Belfast, Ireland, on St. Patrick's Day. In 1870, at just eighteen years old, Patsy made his way to New York on the SS *Marathon* with the hopes of building a prosperous life. He was immediately drawn to the mining industry and had a good intuition for spotting profitable claims.

In 1881, he fell in love with and married the young, elegant and beautiful Mary R. Stack (1861–1948, age eighty-seven), and they had eight children together. The family moved to Spokane in 1887, and Patsy proceeded to build a beautiful home for them. Unfortunately, in 1889, it burned to the ground in one of Spokane's notorious fires.

But Patsy was not deterred. He quickly hired the famous architect Kirkland Cutter and commissioned him to create the fabulous mansion that still stands today. The twelve-thousand-square-foot mansion is made from sandstone imported all the way from Italy, boasting rounded towers, intricately carved gargoyles, Tiffany lamps and chandeliers hauled over from New York, onyx fireplaces, a fourteen-foot-tall-by-eight-foot-wide stained-glass peacock design window and a nine-foot-tall grandfather clock imported from Elliott of London that set Patsy back by $17,000! When all was said and done, the complete and furnished Patsy Clark mansion cost $13 million! (Approximately $100 million in today's prices.)

The mysterious gargoyles that once adorned mining millionaire Patsy Clark's mansion are now gone. Where are the statues now? *Courtesy of LOC #2018699004, Carol M. Highsmith, photographer.*

The 13,700-square-foot Clark Mansion was designed by famous architect Kirtland Cutter in 1898 for the Clark family. Patsy Clark himself haunts his former estate. *Courtesy of author.*

A portrait of Patsy Clark. At the Clark Mansion, people hear the sounds of small children laughing and running through the rooms when none are present. *Courtesy of author.*

The Clarks continued to entertain Spokane's elites in their mansion as their wealth grew and grew. They became prominent citizens in Spokane and were well loved by many. Patsy succumbed to the combination of myocarditis (inflammation of the heart) and "la grippe" (influenza) on June 7, 1915, at one o'clock in the morning, surrounded by his doctor and family. He died peacefully in his mansion at just sixty-four years old.

Mary and her children continued to enjoy living in the mansion until 1926, when they sold it. Mary moved into an apartment building across the street and kept a watchful eye on her mansion. She died in 1948.

The mansion slowly fell into decline and underwent many changes over the years. It was the Francis Lester Inn until 1982. It is said that the paranormal activities started when the estate was remodeled into a restaurant. Many investigators believe the hauntings began as a bit of a rebellion by Mary herself—possibly irritated that her lovely home was being used for something else? Wine bottles were seen floating in the air down in the basement where they were stored. Employees made their way to the basement only reluctantly, frightened of what bizarre and unexplained events they might encounter.

The mansion was facelifted again in 1982 into the Patsy Clark Restaurant, which served the public for another twenty years. Again, the mansion would need extensive repairs. Luckily, the law firm Eyman, Allison, Hunter & Jones lovingly restored the estate to its majestic former glory. Today, the mansion shines on and is an incredible event venue for rent, dazzling everyone who enters its doors.

It seems as though several ghosts haunt the mansion. Who in their right mind would ever want to leave such a beautiful and outstanding estate such as the Patsy Clark mansion—even after their death? Certainly not the Clark family!

NOTE: The Patsy Clark Mansion is located in the Brown's Addition at 2208 West Second Avenue. It is now owned by private individuals, so please enjoy its beauty only from the street. This spectacular estate is available to rent for weddings and special occasions. Please visit https://www.patsyclarkmansion.com.

SPOKANE'S CARNEGIE LIBRARY

The first library in Spokane was just a small room in the old auditorium building, housing a simple twenty pieces of literature that were donated

Spokane's Carnegie Library is haunted by its first head librarian, and many have witnessed a beautiful female ghost peering out the window at the street below. *Courtesy of SPL, 1931.*

by the Spokane Sorosis Club in 1891 and managed by the Union Library Association. A group of adventurous ladies raised the money needed to purchase the first batch of books.

The library relocated to a small, rented space in the basement of City Hall. The good citizens of Spokane realized that their community would embrace a new library, so they submitted a proposal for a grant to the Carnegie Foundation to make their dreams come true.

In 1903, the grant was approved, and preparations began for construction of the new library. The wealthy businessman Andrew Carnegie (1835–1919, age eighty-four) soon donated the funds from his foundation needed for the new building that would be constructed at 10 South Cedar, creating the main branch of the Spokane Public Library. (During the last eighteen years of his life, he gave away around $350 million—roughly $5.9 billion in 2022 and almost 90 percent of his fortune—to charities, foundations and universities.) For the Spokane location, Carnegie donated $85,000 of the $100,000 required for its construction. It is interesting to note that Spokane millionaire Amasa B. Campbell (see "Campbell Mansion" on page 68 generously donated the land needed for the project.

Left: Some wonder if Anna Marie Hardy, a librarian at the Spokane Public Library in the early 1900s, is the mysterious ghost haunting the building. *Courtesy of SPL, 1919.*

Right: Some believe the female spirit haunting the Spokane Public Library is Fay Thomas, who worked in circulation from 1913 until 1920. *Courtesy of SPL.*

The building still stands, although it has been remodeled and updated. Its massive front entry still boasts the original four spectacular columns.

It is rumored that the Carnegie building is haunted by its first head librarian. Many have witnessed a beautiful female ghost peering out the windows at the street below. This ghost is possibly Anna Marie Hardy, who worked in the library in the early 1900s. She was a dedicated employee and really enjoyed working there.

Others believe the female ghost might be the beautiful Fay Thomas, who worked in the library from 1913 to 1920. Both women had striking features and gorgeous eyes, so it is hard to tell which spirit woman is seen peering out the windows. Or could it possibly be both girls—neither wanting to leave the beautiful Spokane Carnegie building?

OLD SPAGHETTI FACTORY

Ghosts from the Prohibition era are believed to haunt the Old Spaghetti Factory restaurant in Spokane. Established in 1890, the building was once used as a liquor warehouse. Some claim to see the ghosts of rumrunners inside the train cargo platform area. Others see apparitions in the kitchen.

What's even more interesting is that multiple Old Spaghetti Factory locations are also haunted!

The Phoenix, Arizona location (1418 North Central Avenue) was formerly a furniture store and a private residence, and locals and staff claim the building has a gloomier, darker past. A female apparition in the basement and an old man floating through the hallways as if looking for someone have both been reported, and diners have heard whispers, screams and sobs and airborne furniture thrown around by an unseen force.

The Old Spaghetti Factory at 1431 Buena Vista Street in Duarte, California, was a high school in the early 1900s, and phantom children's ghosts have reportedly been heard by both employees and guests. Dishes and silverware have been seen falling onto the floor, as if thrown by invisible hands!

In Canada, the Old Spaghetti Factory located at 53 Water Street in Vancouver, British Columbia, eternally houses the restless spirit of a phantom train conductor. Local legend says that his ghost haunts the building because he died in a railway accident—and the actual no. 53 trolley car that's on display in the restaurant was involved in his untimely death.

Can all these Old Spaghetti Factory restaurants be haunted, or is it some sort of marketing ploy? These unique Italian American chain restaurants can offer up more than just delicious pasta for everyone to enjoy. Visit one near you and see if you spot a ghost or two!

NOTE: The Old Spaghetti Factory Restaurant is located at 152 South Monroe Street, Spokane, Washington 99201.

THE SPOKANE FLOATERS

The sad mystery of dozens of corpses found floating in the Spokane River over the years has become an urban legend known as the Spokane Floaters. Dating as far back as 1892, the bodies of locals have been pulled from the icy currents flowing around and through the city of Spokane. Some claim to have seen mysterious lights hovering over the Spokane River, possibly the spirits of those who lost their lives within its murky waters.

Some of these tragic deaths have been suicides, some accidents—and some cold-blooded murders. But is there more to these multiple dark and mysterious (many unsolved) deaths than meets the eye?

In the frigid winter of 1892, the dead body of a man named Thomas Mueraley (also known as LeBaron) was spotted on the south bank of the Spokane River. How did he get there? Did he jump? Was he killed? The case quickly went as cold as his corpse.

Two months later, another body was found floating downstream. On March 2, the body of Peter Allison was discovered in the cloudy waters. A brief investigation ensued, but it was never exposed whether Allison's death was accidental or by design.

The next month, on April 22, Frank Day's body would be pulled out of the river. Some claim he drowned, but others felt foul play was involved.

In June, Arthur Carson's body was seen floating in the Spokane River. Authorities were called out once again, but no in-depth investigation was undertaken and no final determination was made.

In the fall, the whirlpools of the Spokane River took yet another victim. C.D. Ebert was seen praying by the bridge. Then a nearby citizen, Albert Anderson, witnessed him jumping headlong into the icy waters of the lower falls near the Monroe Street Bridge. Why did he jump? Anderson

Spokane's Monroe Street Bridge is haunted by several of the victims who have lost their lives in the turbulent waters below. *Courtesy of LOC #2014690144, Bain News Service, Publisher, 1910.*

quickly ran to the police to notify them of the suicide. The officers grabbed their special ropes, ones made especially for the grisly task of retrieving victims from the river. (The ropes had strong metal hooks attached to them, allowing bodies to be easily pulled from the water.) The police hung their special ropes over the bridge, trying in vain for many hours to locate, hook and grasp the victim. But when the sun set, they decided to give up on the task.

The chilly waters of the Spokane River still continue to lure and claim victims. Over the years, dozens of people have been found floating in the river. Is the Spokane River cursed? Why do so many people feel the desire to leap to their deaths? Is there some sort of magnetic pull that tempts and appeals to those experiencing tough times? Or could it be even more sinister? Perhaps the river is simply a well-known, dumping ground where killers dispose of their victims.

THE GHOST OF CHARLES CANNING

Murder is probably one of the most harrowing experiences a person and their loved ones, family and friends can endure. Maybe that is why a significant percentage of paranormal activities revolve around these traumatic events. Ghosts tend to linger where they died or were killed. Do they wish to seek revenge? Or are they waiting around for their murderer's identity to be brought to light so they can move on? No one really knows why spirits tend to hang out at certain locations or buildings, but that would be a good assumption.

One such violent murder involved Charles Canning, whose own good friend, Andrew O'Conner, killed him in cold blood. O'Conner had been the chief of police in Cleveland, Ohio, for several years before his family moved to Spokane, where he was now earning $4.20 per day in wages. In the late 1800s, that was considered decent money.

Mrs. O'Conner had a boardinghouse on the corner of Division Street and Riverside Avenue, and Charles Canning worked as her dishwasher. The O'Conners had been married seventeen years, and Mrs. O'Conner often complained to people about how badly her husband treated her. "He often threatened to torture me to death because I didn't want to wait on him," she told police. During the time of the tragedy, the O'Conners had temporarily split up, and Mrs. O'Conner had become smitten with Canning. Mr. O'Conner began to suspect that his wife and Canning were sleeping

Looking south on Stevens Street from Main Street in Spokane (1912), where Andrew O'Conner, in a jealous rage, killed Charles Canning in cold blood in 1890. *Courtesy of SPL.*

together when he was away on business in Seattle, Washington, and rumors began to circulate around town about their torrid affair—rumors that were quickly shared with Mr. O'Conner.

But Mrs. O'Conner denied any intimacy between herself and Canning.

Canning had already been tossed in jail for thirty days for fighting with Mr. O'Conner, but (going against the social standards of the time) Mrs.

O'Conner quickly bailed him out of jail, and he was released. Little did she know she should have left him safely behind bars. Why would the wife of another man supply Canning's bail money if they weren't intimately involved? The world would soon find out.

Just a few days prior to Canning's death, on September 22, 1890, Mrs. O'Conner had been arrested for attempting to murder Mr. O'Conner with a flatiron (with the help of an unknown male companion, possibly Canning). But nothing seems to have come from her arrest except a stern warning.

The fighting between the two men resumed on September 25. They would argue and fight every time they crossed paths. One fight got so violent that Canning struck Mr. O'Conner on the head with a rock.

The fateful evening of the murder, around eight thirty, O'Conner, consumed by a jealous rage, hid behind some bushes waiting for Canning to walk by, his gun nearby, ready for action. As Canning walked along, he approached the corner of Main and Stevens Streets, oblivious to the fact that he would soon be a dead man.

O'Conner jumped out and raised his personal six-chamber No. 45 Colt Single Action Army revolver and aimed it directly at Canning's head. "You are a God damn son of a bitch!" he yelled and pulled the trigger.

The bullet struck Canning behind his left ear and exited out his right temple. There was no chance of survival. Policeman Olmstead witnessed the whole incident, along with countless other civilians walking along Main Street that night. He quickly grabbed O'Conner and took the weapon from him. Soon, Sergeant McKernan and Captain Coverly were at the bloody scene.

"My God, Andy, what have you done?" cried Coverly.

"If I hadn't shot him, I should have committed suicide. I am nearly crazy!" was O'Conner's answer.

O'Conner was swept off to prison to deal with his fate. Spokane Undertaking Company was called, and they soon arrived to take Canning's corpse to the morgue.

Does the spirit of Charles Canning still roam Main Street in Spokane, seeking revenge for his untimely death? It is highly likely. Some claim to see the ghostly figure of a man wearing a boiler hat late at night near the area where Canning died.

SPOKANE UFOS

Spokane and its surrounding areas have long been known to experience dozens of reported UFO sightings over the years. These reports typically involve descriptions of unidentified lights or strange objects exhibiting unusual flight characteristics that defy all conventional explanations. Some witnesses have reported seeing weird objects that appear to move in ways not consistent with any known aircraft.

In July 1952, there were multiple accounts of UFO sightings in the Spokane area. Witnesses described seeing bright, fast-moving lights in the night sky. Stories of these sightings were quickly snatched up and published by local reporters.

On August 1 that same year, so many people reported UFO sightings over Spokane that the *Spokane Chronicle* wrote up a story on it. About 7:00 p.m., Bill King and several of his friends spotted a star-shaped, silver object flying over Spokane, heading toward Coeur d'Alene, Idaho. A man named Ray Bruner saw a baseball-size object hovering over Napa Street at about 7:15 p.m. A Mrs. Bertolino and her daughter were driving nearby when they saw a flying object about 9:45 the next morning. The daughter told reporters, "I was downtown in a car at Sprague and Bernard when my mother looked up in the sky and saw this object. It was a shining light, not very big, which looked something like a spoon. It was just floating along, not moving fast." Mrs. Bertolino's mother, Mrs. Benjamin Hall, also saw the strange object.

So what exactly is haunting us from the skies? Are the small, baseball-size flying objects paranormal orbs of energy? Are the larger UFOs from another dimension of space and time, or are they actual aircraft with aliens on board?

CHIEF QUALCHAN'S AND CHIEF OWHI'S VICIOUS MURDERS

The hanging of Chief Qualchan took place along a section of Hangman Creek (also known as Latah Creek, the water runs sixty miles from the Rocky Mountains to the Spokane River). Chief Qualchan was hanged as a result of his resistance against the intrusion of unwanted White settlers who were taking over land in Yakama territory. Some people consider the area by Hangman's Creek an active paranormal spot due to its violent past. The residual energy left behind from a traumatic event can often keep a building or location filled with restless spirits.

The trouble started brewing between the Native Americans and the White settlers in 1858, when the first governor of Washington Territory, Isaac Stevens, forced the tribes to sign treaties surrendering their land, freedom and beliefs over to the settlers. Most of the Natives were resentful and angry over the unfairness and were ready to go to battle to keep their fertile and productive land for themselves.

But the United States government refused to accept the Natives' rebuttals, and the U.S. Army quickly dispatched six hundred troops under the command of Colonel George Wright to overcome the Indian tribes of Eastern Washington by "any means necessary"—even if that meant death.

Wright and his troops began marching north from Fort Walla Walla. Soon, they were approached and halted by several cautious Native tribes, at both Four Lakes and Spokane Plains. Angered by the Natives' stubborn refusal to accept the new terms, Wright decided to stop at the Spokane River (the area of present-day Liberty Lake) to determine his next move.

His next move proved horrendous. On September 8, Wright ordered the bloody, unnecessary slaughter of almost one thousand horses that belonged to the Palouse tribe. Even Wright's own soldiers were sickened by the sight of the innocent horses being killed. Wright figured this was the fastest (and cruelest) way to get the attention and cooperation of the Palouse. Many of the soldiers wrote to their loved ones that they would never scrub the horrendous sight of the slaughter from their minds or the sounds of the screaming horses from their memories.

But why did Wright want to anger these local Native Americans so much? He wrongly believed that Yakama subchief Qualchan and others of the tribe were attacking White settlers in the area—and were responsible for the murder of United States Indian agent A.J. Bolon in 1855. (It was later determined that Qualchan and the others were nowhere near the area where Bolon was killed. (For more on Bolon, see page 135.)

But the bull-headed Wright remained determined, and he demanded Qualchan be given the status of a wanted fugitive by territorial authorities. On September 23, 1858, desperate for peace, Qualchan's father, Chief Owhi, rode into Wright's camp carrying a white flag signaling their surrender. But Owhi was immediately placed in restraints. Wright wanted to hold him hostage in order to lure his son Qualchan to the camp.

The next day, Qualchan and his wife, Whist-alks; his son; and two other warriors (including his brother Lo-kout) rode their horses to the camp in hopes of making peace. He was completely unaware that his father had been taken captive and was being held against his will.

In 1858, Chief Owhi was killed while being held prisoner at Fort Walla Walla. When Owhi made a break for freedom and began running away, Sergeant Ball killed him. *Drawing courtesy of author.*

But again, Wright refused to negotiate or accept their surrender. Instead, he ordered Qualchan to be captured and hanged without a trial. The nervous Qualchan looked around the camp and soon saw his father Owhi bound and restrained nearby. He knew in his heart that the White men had yet again deceived them.

Soldiers were ordered to assault and restrain Qualchan while others set up a makeshift gallows in a nearby tree. Qualchan was an extraordinarily strong warrior, and it was difficult for the soldiers to subdue him. But in the end, brute force overcame Qualchan, and he was slowly strangled to death. As he died, he placed a curse on Wright and his soldiers. His distraught wife fought desperately to save her husband, but she was unable to defend him against the soldiers.

Later that night, Wright wrote of the day in his journal: "Qualchan came to see me at 9 o'clock, and at 9:15 he was hung." After his death was verified, Qualchan's body was brought down, stripped naked and buried in a shallow grave by the river's edge.

Chief Owhi was held prisoner and taken south to Fort Walla Walla, his feet tied together under the belly of a horse in hopes that this would keep him restrained. When the soldiers guarding him stopped for water at a stream,

Owhi made a break for freedom and began running away. Lieutenant Michael R. Morgan ran Owhi down, then ordered Sergeant Edward Ball to kill him. Ball obeyed his orders, placed his pistol to the warrior's head and quickly pulled the trigger several times.

Later, as a death trophy, Owhi's saddle was given to Surgeon General Joseph Barnes.

Over three days, another dozen or so Native Americans were also hanged, all without a proper trial. Qualchan's death was only the beginning of what could be considered a hanging spree by the bloodthirsty Wright.

The angry spirits of Owhi and Qualchan still haunt the area once known as Hangman Creek. Some claim to hear heartbreaking phantom cries from the ghost of Whist-alks, forever mourning the loss of her beloved husband.

NOTE: To learn more about the history and ghosts of Spokane, please read *Ghosts and Legends of Spokane* by Deborah Cuyle from The History Press.

CHENEY

Just a few miles from Spokane is a town called Cheney, home to a few active spirits.

Cheney was officially incorporated on November 28, 1883, and it owes its name to Benjamin Pierce Cheney, a Boston railroad tycoon. In the late 1860s and early 1870s, settlers were drawn to Cheney due to its plentiful water, abundant timber and the promise of a new railway line. The area had seen Native American unrest during the territorial period, but eventually, homes were established near where the Burlington Northern depot now stands.

Cheney is now home to Eastern Washington University (EWU), a public regional university with over ten thousand full-time students.

Over thirteen thousand people call Cheney their hometown today. With plenty of local shops, parks, the Cheney Historical Museum, the Turnbull National Wildlife Refuge, breweries and restaurants, Cheney has a mix of outdoor beauty, historical charm and local gems just waiting to be explored.

But first, let's take a look at Cheney's fascinating local haunts.

ELIZABETH McLANAHAN'S IRRITATING SPIRIT

Back in 1909, a woman named Elizabeth C. McLanahan (1849–1924, age seventy-five) became so irritated by and scared of a spirit living in her small cottage that she actually placed flyers around town offering a $15 reward (about $500 today) to anyone who could get rid of the ghost. Now, considering she was a widow trying to support herself on the wages of a laundress, that was a pretty hefty sum to offer up.

What exactly was the ghost doing to bother the woman so much? It must have been obnoxious, because she even contacted a reporter for the *Spokesman-Review* and pleaded for them to print up her reward.

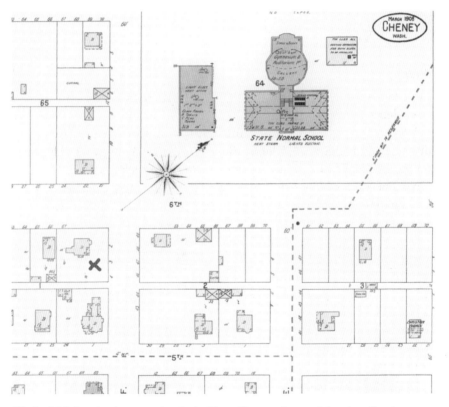

Elizabeth McLanahan's cottage (marked with an *X*) was so haunted that she offered a reward of $15 (about $500 today) to anyone who could get rid of the ghost! *Courtesy of LOC #sanborn09134_007, Sandborn Map of Cheney in 1908.*

She wrote:

Fifteen dollars reward will be paid to anyone that will locate and identify a party prowling around my back door and yard and kitchen windows evenings from near 7 till 9 o'clock. A view may be had from both streets and alley. This is not a freak of imagination. The sneak does exist, but is ghostlike, as he seems to float out and near and does not seem to wear any shoes. Signed, Mrs. E.C. M'Lanahan.

The ghost had been bothering her for months. Her little cottage was located at 321 Sixth Street on the corner of Sixth and F Streets, catty-corner from the Cheney State Normal School. She was living alone with only the company of the ghost, as her husband, William, had died in 1893.

Elizabeth eventually sold the house in 1917, and she moved back to her birth state, Pennsylvania, to stay with her family. She had progressive spinal muscular atrophy and needed special care and someone to watch over her.

Her cottage was torn down, and apartments were built on her old lot. Some locals claim the apartment building is haunted now, too, but there is no evidence to support that.

A cenotaph marker for Elizabeth stands in the Fairview Cemetery, although she is not buried there. She is buried in Pennsylvania alongside her parents at the Rocky Glenn Cemetery in Adamsville, Crawford County.

No one ever claimed the fifteen-dollar reward, and Elizabeth's ghost seems to have never left Cheney.

EASTERN WASHINGTON UNIVERSITY

It seems as though most old universities house a ghost or two. Perhaps these stories are just created by overtired imaginations—or are the scary stories real?

Eastern Washington University (EWU) was formerly the Cheney State Normal School. After the original Benjamin P. Cheney Academy (which served as the precursor to the normal school) tragically burned down in August 1891, the community rallied together. Despite setbacks, they eventually secured funding to rebuild. In 1895, the state legislature finally approved funds for a new building, and the cornerstone for this new

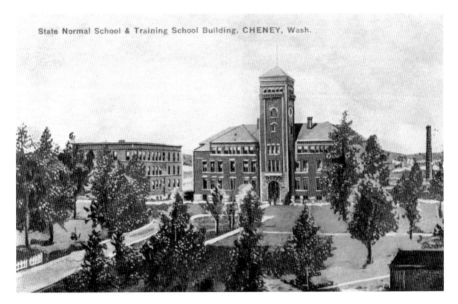

State Normal School & Training School Building. CHENEY, Wash.

The former Cheney State Normal School (now on the campus of Eastern Washington University) has ghosts haunting several of its halls. *Courtesy of WSA.*

normal school was laid on October 15, 1895, during a grand ceremony attended by many.

The new normal school officially opened its doors for classes in October 1896. The brick-clad wooden structure featured a granite foundation and a front entry made of quarried stone from Medical Lake. Inside, it boasted modern equipment, new separate classrooms (instead of one big classroom, as before), laboratories and a large library on the first floor. But tragedy would strike again…

Late in the evening on April 24, 1912, another fire engulfed the school, trapping two teachers, Mr. Wert and Mr. Miranda, in their third-floor tower room. As smoke poured into the room, the teachers jumped out the windows to safety outside.

The exact cause of the fire remains unknown. It initially started in the basement of the main building and quickly spread.

Firefighters improvised, using a carpet from a nearby home to catch Mr. Wert as he jumped to safety.

Unfortunately, Mr. Miranda sustained injuries during his leap, but he eventually recovered. By two thirty in the morning, the walls of the building were still standing, but the interior was a total loss. The damage was estimated to be worth around $400,000.

Despite the devastation, the resilient spirit of EWU prevailed. Classes continued in homes, churches and other available spaces while plans for rebuilding were organized.

The Cheney Normal School continued to evolve over the years. It transformed into the Eastern Washington College of Education in 1937, then became Eastern Washington State College in 1961. Finally, in 1977, it adopted its current name: Eastern Washington University. The original core of the university campus (including the six oldest buildings) is part of the Washington State Normal School in the Cheney Historic District. These historic structures, along with the iconic herculean pillars at the traditional entryway, have been on the National Register of Historic Places since 1992.

Several halls are known to be haunted at EWU.

SHOWALTER HALL: This historic building is rumored to be haunted by the ghost of a former student named Dorothy, who tragically died in a fire. Visitors have reported hearing footsteps and strange noises and feeling an eerie presence in the hallways at night.

SUTTON HALL: Another prominent building on campus, Sutton Hall, is said to be haunted by the spirit of a maintenance worker who passed away while working there. Some claim to have seen his apparition late at night, performing his duties as if he never left.

THE GHOSTLY PIANIST: There have been accounts of a phantom pianist playing haunting melodies in the practice rooms of the Music Building. However, upon investigation, no one is ever found playing the piano.

DRYDEN HALL: Rumors of a male apparition persist, and the ghost is mainly active on the second floor. Some claim a young student committed suicide in Dryden Hall in the 1960s and that his spirit is the one attached to the building.

THE LADY IN WHITE: A spectral woman dressed in white has been spotted near the university's library. She is often seen wandering the grounds, especially during foggy evenings. Some believe she might be a former student or faculty member.

MONROE HALL: The Monroe Hall elevator is notorious for its eerie behavior. Students have reported strange occurrences, such as the elevator stopping on random floors even when no buttons are pressed. Some claim to have heard whispers or felt cold drafts inside. Monroe Hall was built in 1916.

NOTE: Eastern Washington University is located at 526 Fifth Street in Cheney. Please do not disrupt the school, its staff or its students.

CHAPTER 2

MIDDLE EASTERN REGION

ELLENSBURG TO COLFAX AND EVERYTHING IN BETWEEN

ELLENSBURG

The first American pioneers settled in the area around 1868. William "Bud" Wilson built the first log cabin, and cowboys A.J. Splawn and Ben Burch opened a general store called Robber's Roost in 1870. John A. Shoudy, a Civil War veteran, purchased the store and land in 1872 and later started a postal service in Ellensburg. He platted an eighty-acre section of land for the town on July 20, 1875, and named it Ellensburgh after his wife, Mary Ellen. By 1883, Ellensburg had grown significantly, with a bank, a fire company, a newspaper and soon, a population of 2,768. Next it became the county seat of Kittitas County. The arrival of the Northern Pacific Railroad in the 1880s fueled rapid growth. Ellensburg was even a leading candidate to become the state capital of Washington. However, a devastating fire on July 4, 1889, destroyed most of the city. Despite this setback, Ellensburg quickly rebuilt, with brick buildings replacing wooden ones. The city purchased its private electric lighting system in 1890, and the post office changed the spelling of the city's name to Ellensburg in 1894.

During Prohibition (1920–33), speakeasies cropped up in Ellensburg, as they did in many other places in the United States. These hidden, illegal bars operated secretly, serving much-wanted alcohol to willing patrons.

Ellensburg continued to grow and prosper over the years. Today, almost twenty thousand people enjoy living in the city. The Kittitas County Historical Museum, housed in the historic 1889 Cadwell Building, offers exhibits spanning the history of Kittitas County. You can explore Native American beadwork and learn about local pioneers and their families, local farming, mining and logging and lots more. It's a fascinating journey through the region's past.

Ellensburg is renowned for its exciting rodeo events. The Ellensburg Rodeo is a highlight of the year and draws rodeo enthusiasts from far and wide. It features thrilling competitions, including bull riding, steer wrestling, barrel racing and more. The grand parade, carnival rides and live music add to the festive atmosphere.

But lurking in dark corners and historical buildings, a few interactive ghosts keep Ellensburg even more interesting!

BEN SNIPES HAUNTED BANK

The Wells Fargo bank in Ellensburg is reportedly haunted—but by whom? Lights flicker on and off for no reason, heavy objects are moved by unseen hands, the sounds of heavy sighs come from invisible lips and, once in a while, the apparition of a male figure is seen peering out through its windows.

But who is this male spirit? No one really knows.

The Wells Fargo bank in Ellensburg is haunted, but by whom? It was formerly the Ben Snipes bank, which hosted a horse show in 1889, pictured here. *Courtesy of Ellensburg Public Library.*

Ben Snipes's small cabin was built in 1859 and was disassembled, moved and reassembled at Sunnyside Museum in 1968. *Courtesy of WSA, Werner Lenggenhager, photographer.*

One guess might be that it is the ghost of a prominent Ellensburg pioneer who was much loved and an inspiration to many. Ben Elliott Snipes (1835–1906, age seventy-one) was a devilishly handsome fellow who was born in North Carolina. He made his way to Iowa with his family in 1847. When he was just seventeen years of age, he joined a wagon train headed west to Oregon. He began working on a cattle ranch and, realizing how much he loved it, decided he, too, was going to become a cattle rancher. He headed toward Eastern Washington around 1887 and slowly made his dream a reality. With good business sense and some luck, Snipes acquired a fairly decent fortune, although he remained a very humble man, living modestly.

But the harsh winters and financial troubles faced by many people also affected Snipes, and he lost most of his money. He was determined not to give up or give in. No matter what obstacle he faced, he continued on with his plans.

Snipes built the first bank in Ellensburg in 1888 and another bank in Roslyn, Washington. The first horse show in Ellensburg was conducted in front of his bank in the fall of 1888 on the southeast corner of Pearl Street and Fifth Avenue. His Ellensburg bank was called the Ben Snipes & Co. Bank, and a massive fire burned it down in 1889. Again, Snipes was not deterred, and he rebuilt his bank that very same year.

Snipes's Roslyn bank has an even more interesting past. In 1892, the Butch Cassidy gang arrived, and the five men robbed the bank of between $5,000 and $10,000. (The sum reported varies.)

Snipes continued his cattle business in 1896 and had even acquired one thousand horses by 1897. His business ventures continued to have ups and downs, but Snipes always kept up a positive outlook on life. At times, he had to sell off assets or animals to get his debts paid, but he never skipped out on money owed.

The Snipes family eventually moved to Seattle, Washington, around 1899, where they would live out their days. Mr. Snipes died of pneumonia at seventy-one years old.

His bank was remodeled in the 1940s and is now a Wells Fargo Bank branch. Employees claim it has two resident ghosts. It wouldn't be a stretch to think that Mr. Ben Snipes himself is still protecting his assets by hanging around his old bank.

NOTE: The Wells Fargo Bank in Ellensburg is located at 104 East Fourth Avenue, Ellensburg, Washington 98926.

LIBERTY THEATER

At the Liberty Theater in Ellensburg, many people have heard weird sounds and phantom screaming at night. Some have also reported the bathroom doors randomly opening and closing. Why would a ghost haunt a bathroom?

The Liberty Theater was opened in 1940 and operated by Midstate Amusement Corporation. It is a striking example of Streamline Moderne architecture, and its exterior resembles the bridge of an ocean liner, complete with a tall rectangular vertical marquee and service ladders that enhance the nautical impression. Inside, the theater boasted a comfortably modern design.

Unfortunately, the Liberty Theater closed in August 2009. In 2010, it underwent a transformation and became a church.

The identity of the entity haunting the Liberty Theater remains shrouded in mystery. Perhaps it is a restless spirit from the theater's past, drawn to its historic architecture and memories of bygone movie screenings. Or maybe it's a former employee who made the theater their favorite hangout.

Whatever the case, the ghostly presence adds an extra layer of intrigue to this iconic building.

NOTE: The Liberty Theater is located at 111 East Fifth Avenue, Ellensburg, Washington, 98926.

THE GHOST OF KAMOLA HALL

The spirit of a girl named Lola haunts the Kamola Hall of Central Washington University (CWU) in Ellensburg, but nobody really knows why. Many have witnessed her apparition and heard her phantom voice.

Everyone says that Lola is a friendly ghost, and she likes to play fun little tricks on people. Her phantom footsteps can often be heard walking up and down the halls, and she is often seen wearing a white dress.

But who is Lola? Why does she haunt Kamola Hall? Again, no one knows. Students gave her the nickname Lola Kamola—but is her name really Lola? Students claim to see her ghost so often that they talk to her just as if she were a living being!

The college proudly opened its doors on September 6, 1891. Kamola Hall, located on the south end of campus on University Way, was built in 1920 and is the second-oldest building on campus and the first residence hall

Kamola Hall at Central Washington University (pictured when it was the Washington Normal School) holds the playful spirit of a little girl named Lola. *Courtesy of WSA, Delong & Drake, photographer.*

built at CWU. Today, it has been renovated to accommodate students who are attending college there.

Some speculate that Lola lived on campus in the 1920s. Legend says that her lover was killed in World War I and she was so distraught that she hanged herself on the fourth floor. Others claim she died during the 1940s, as they have seen the apparition wearing dresses from that era.

It is interesting to note that on August 16, 1947, a woman named Miss Ruth Woods (who was acting dean of the college) died unexpectedly of a heart attack after entering Kamola Hall on her way to her apartment. Woods was only forty-six years old and had been a teacher for twenty-four years— so she started teaching when she was just twenty-two years old. Woods had a passion for her career, so perhaps it is actually her spirit that haunts Kamola Hall. Maybe her untimely death has caused her to hang around the hall where she once was so happy and productive? That would make sense!

NOTE: Central Washington University is located at 400 East University Way, Ellensburg, Washington 98926. Please do not disturb the university, staff or students.

ELLENSBURG PUBLIC LIBRARY

Some claim to see the ghost of a former director, Celeste Kline, who worked at the library for many years before her passing in 2005. It is said that Kline loved the library and devoted her life to making it perfect. She worked tirelessly to make sure the library was always in tip-top shape and superbly organized. Over the years since her departure, people have claimed to see her spirit and experience unusual activity. Does Kline still roam her library, making sure it is still running smoothly and everything is as it should be? Some say yes.

NOTE: The Ellensburg Public Library is located at 209 North Ruby Street, Ellensburg, Washington 98926. Please do not disturb the staff or disrupt the building.

ROSLYN

Roslyn was founded in 1886 as a coal mining company town by Logan M. Bullitt, who was the vice president of the Northern Pacific Coal Company. The town's establishment coincided with the discovery of coal and the arrival of the Northern Pacific Railroad in 1886. Bullitt played a crucial role in naming the town, choosing the name Roslyn after a faraway town in Delaware where his sweetheart lived.

Roslyn's roots are deeply tied to the coal industry, which played a significant role in shaping the town's early history. Between 1886 and 1929, immigrant workers from various countries arrived in Roslyn to work in the coal mines. They hailed from places like Italy, Poland, Slovakia, Germany, Lithuania, Slovenia, Serbia, Croatia, England, Ireland, Scotland and Wales. The traditions and cultural heritage of these immigrant miners are still evident today. The Roslyn Cemetery reflects the diversity of these early settlers, with distinct ethnic and lodge sections.

Roslyn reached its peak coal mine production of nearly two million tons in 1910. The coal was essential for railway construction and operations, but as steam trains transitioned to diesel power, the mines gradually closed down in the 1920s.

Roslyn gained some fame as the filming location for several popular TV shows and movies, such as *Northern Exposure* (an iconic 1990s television show set in the fictional town of Cicely, Alaska, but primarily filmed in Roslyn), *The Man in the High Castle* and *The Runner Stumbles*.

Many of Roslyn's historical buildings have been meticulously preserved. The downtown area boasts false-front wooden buildings reminiscent of an Old West town. In recognition of its historical significance, Roslyn's downtown was added to the National Register of Historic Places in 1978.

Roslyn's unique charm and historical architecture make it a wonderful place to stop on your way through or for a fun day trip. Although only around one thousand people live in Roslyn, its historical significance, picturesque surroundings and cultural heritage continue to attract residents and visitors alike.

The town also attracts a few uninvited guests—local ghosts!

THE BRICK SALOON

The Brick Saloon in Roslyn is the oldest continuously operated saloon in Washington State and houses both kinds of spirits: alcohol and ghosts! It is reportedly haunted by several entities, including the ghost of a little girl and a lone cowboy. There is a piano in the back room that often plays all by itself. Often, the sound of phantom firewood being split can be heard.

John Buffo and Peter Giovanni (who was also the town's mayor) operated a small saloon on the site of the current Brick Saloon. It was rebuilt in 1889 (the same year Washington became a state) using a whopping forty-five thousand bricks (thus the bar's name). The bar back (the ornate wooden fixture behind a bar that all of the booze is displayed on) came all the way from England, and the twenty-six-foot-long running-water spittoon was installed in 1889 by (and for) the local miners. The local miners often chewed tobacco instead of smoking it because their lungs were already compromised by their job. The historic spittoon is still running today, although the city has been trying to shut it down for years for some reason.

The tavern gained some fame as the set of the fictional Holling's Bar in the television series *Northern Exposure*. (*Northern Exposure* was an American comedy-drama TV series about the eccentric residents of a fictional small town in Alaska that ran on CBS from 1990 to 1995 for a total of 110 episodes. The show was nominated for fifty-seven awards during its five-year run and won twenty-seven of them.)

The Brick Saloon gained a bit more acclaim when it was used as the courtroom set in Stanley Kramer's *The Runner Stumbles*.

Besides ghostly apparitions, the Brick also experiences objects moving and cold spots. One former bartender got so freaked out by the paranormal activity that he quit his job on the spot, walking out of the tavern never to return to the site.

Whether or not this historic saloon is actually haunted, it's definitely a wonderful place to enjoy a cold beer and a hot meal in a great atmosphere.

Notes: The ghostly male entity that lingers at the Brick may stem from a terrible tragedy that occurred in 1945. A man who worked in Roslyn for two decades as a tavern operator committed suicide on June 18. Frank Cuculich (1880–1945, age fifty-eight) walked into an unnamed Roslyn tavern at nine thirty in the morning and greeted Joe Briggs, the bartender at the tavern Frank operated. He announced calmly, "Goodbye, Joe. Inform my sister." Then he walked into the back room, put a revolver to his head and pulled the trigger. (It is unclear exactly which tavern he conducted his suicide at.) Perhaps his restless spirit still roams the town he once loved so much. No one ever discovered why Frank killed himself. Maybe he haunts the Brick because it is a familiar, friendly and comfortable atmosphere and it just feels like home to him.

The Brick Saloon is located at 100 West Pennsylvania Avenue, Roslyn, Washington 98941. Stop in for a bite to eat and a cold beer—maybe you will experience some paranormal activity yourself!

HISTORIC ROSLYN CEMETERIES

Roslyn's historic cemeteries—the final resting place for thousands of souls since 1887—play a significant role in preserving and commemorating the town's history. Some claim to witness shadowy figures and strange noises coming from the cemetery late at night—when no one should be around...

The town prides itself on its ginormous group of cemeteries, the historical aspects of which are fascinating. The acreage houses twenty-six separate cemeteries where people of over twenty-four different nationalities are buried. With over five thousand graves, one can conclude that there is a spirit or two roaming the massive fifteen acres.

The Roslyn Cemetery is the largest and most well-known; it was established in the late 1800s and serves as the final resting place for many of the town's early residents, including many coal miners and their families. One of the notable features of the Roslyn Cemetery is the presence of numerous headstones and monuments that reflect the diverse ethnic and cultural backgrounds of the various people who settled in the area.

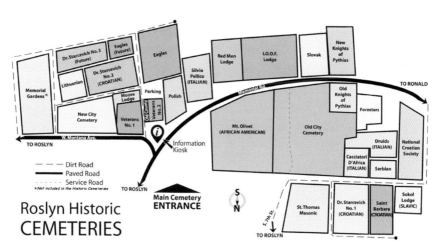

The Roslyn Historic Cemeteries are twenty-seven separate cemeteries where people of over twenty-four different nationalities are buried. With over five thousand graves, this massive complex is the town's pride and joy. *Courtesy of Wikipedia Commons free to share.*

The Masonic Cemetery is the oldest of the cemeteries, with at least one grave dating to 1886. The cemetery is divided into various sections, including a Catholic section, a Jewish section and a section for fraternal organizations like the Independent Order of Odd Fellows (IOOF).

The City Cemetery, also known as the Coal Miner's Cemetery, is another historic burial ground. This cemetery is significant because it contains the graves of many coal miners who played a pivotal role in the coal mining industry that once thrived in Roslyn. Symbols and inscriptions related to mining are carved into their headstones.

The complex has several ethnic sections as well, such as the Italian Cemetery and the Croatian Cemetery. These ethnic cemeteries provide a unique glimpse into the cultural heritage of the various immigrant communities that contributed to the growth and development of Roslyn. The beautiful and historical cemetery complex is well worth visiting when you are in Roslyn.

NOTE: For a more in-depth look at the cemeteries' incredible history and those who are buried there, take a look at:

The Historical Cemeteries of Roslyn, Washington, by Karyne Ware, published on September 30, 2016, and available at: https://issuu.com/roslyncemeteries/docs/roslyncemeteries-karen.

Or https://en.wikipedia.org/wiki/Roslyn_Historical_Cemeteries.

You can contact the cemetery at PO Box 156, Roslyn, Washington 98941 or (509) 649-3105.

ROSLYN'S WORST MINING DISASTER

Some claim that the restless souls of miners who were killed in an instant one day still roam the streets of Roslyn, forever searching for their wives and children.

The morning of May 10, 1892, started out as any other. During these tough times, many families were just grateful to be working—even in the harsh and dangerous conditions deep underground.

The forty-five men who entered the Northern Pacific Coal Company's No. 1 coal mine that day had no idea it would be their last. A heavy rain that seemed to refuse to let up only made matters worse. The mud made the job even more unbearable. These men were already forced to work ten-hour shifts of backbreaking manual labor in horrible conditions. Breaking up and

In 1892, a mining disaster took the lives of forty-five men, leaving the town blanketed in sorrow for years. These unidentified men and mules exhibit the dangerous mining conditions of the era. *Courtesy of LOC #2018673770, Lewis Wickes, photographer.*

hauling coal for ten hours at a time with only a small candle flame to see by seems insane in today's world. Yet these men suffered through day after day for a meager wage of one to three dollars per day. Mine No. 1 had seven levels and went an incredible 2,700 feet below the surface.

Halfway through the long shift, a horrific gas explosion blasted in the mine that could be heard for miles around. Wives, mothers, lovers, sisters, brothers, children and family members all froze in their tracks, for that deafening sound meant only one thing: death.

Immediately, people began running to the mine, praying their loved ones were safe from the blast.

For the men who were trapped in the mine, the clock was ticking. Some were killed instantly, and others had to suffer tragically until they succumbed due to lack of oxygen. The shaft was full of fire, smoke and debris blocking the exits and tunnels.

Outside, men had to use brute force to keep frantic family members from entering the mine in search of their loved ones. In an instant, so many lives were taken: the horrible accident created twenty-nine widows and ninety-one orphans. Several families filed suit against the Northern Pacific Coal

Company, and some of the parties settled, with just $1,000 going to each widow (except if the family had a working-age son; then the payment was lowered to $500).

As rescue efforts slowly continued, the bodies were taken in wagons to the town hall, where they were laid out on tables side by side so that they could be viewed and identified.

A few days after the explosion, funeral services began. The procession for the men was attended by countless people; it was one of the largest the town had seen. Members of the Knights of Pythias, the Independent Order of Odd Fellows (IOOF) and the Sons of Good Templars (SOGT) as well as the Masons—all dressed in full regalia—were in attendance.

The work of excavating the ground for so many graves continued day and night. The sound of dynamite blasts filled the air, rattling survivors' nerves. (The dynamite was being used to expedite the unplanned work of digging forty-five graves in a short time.)

After research was conducted, the state inspector of mines concluded that the mining blast on the morning of May 10 had occurred because something "opened a crack to a pocket of gas and…a miner's lamp on the slope side set off the explosion."

The forty-five miners killed were: Joseph Bennett, Dominio Bianco, John Bowen, Thomas Brennan, George Brooks, Joseph Browitt, Henry Campbell, Tobias Cooper, Joseph Cusworth Jr., Joseph Cusworth Sr., Herman Daister, Phillip D. Davis, Andrew Erlandson, George Forsythe, Richard Forsythe, John Foster, Scott Giles, Robert Graham, William Hague, Mitchell Hale, Frank Haney, John Hodgson, Thomas Holmes, James Huston, Elisha Jackson, John Lafferty, J.D. Lewis, Preston Loving, John Mattias, Daniel McLellan, James Morgan, George Moses, Benjamin Ostliff, William Palmer, William Penhall, Leslie Pollard, David Rees, Thomas Rees, William Robinson, Mitchell Ronald, Robert Spotts, Winyard Steele, Jacob Weatherley, G.M. Williams and Sydney Wright. Rest in peace.

The residual energy from violent or tragic accidents can cause spirits to be trapped in between realms. Hopefully, the men who lost their lives are at peace knowing their story is not forgotten—and neither are they. They are an integral and important part of Roslyn and local mining history.

ROSLYN'S 1909 MINING DISASTER

Although it was not as deadly as the 1892 explosion, during Roslyn's 1909 mining disaster, twelve men were tragically killed. On Sunday, October 3, at 12:45 p.m., an explosion rocked the Northwest Implement Company's No. 4 mine. (NWIC was a subsidiary of the Northern Pacific Railroad that operated a number of mines in both Roslyn and Cle Elum.)

The horrific explosion resonated throughout the entire mine, and fire soon ensued. No one knew for sure, but the men safe outside figured the explosion originated either inside the mine or in the shaft. Flames shot up through the main entrance and spiraled as high as four hundred feet into the air. The blast destroyed the headframe, the tipple (a structure used at a mine to load the extracted product, such as coal or ores, for transport) and snowsheds and the nearby powerhouse. Several other structures also caught fire and burned. Reports claim that the blast was so strong it broke the windows of buildings that were a half a mile away.

A search party was quickly formed, composed of six brave men: Peter Bagley, Arthur Hodder, William Farrington, John Graham, Harry Whiting and Frank Goode. But rescue efforts were futile, and two of the trapped men were never found. Even as the search party fought their way to try to find the victims, poisonous gases soon overwhelmed them as well, threatening their lives. For a long forty-eight hours, water was poured into the shaft in hopes of extinguishing any remaining flames.

On hearing the news, hundreds of men began saying their prayers. Typically, five to six hundred men worked in the mine every day, but Sunday was a maintenance shift, so relatively few workers were on duty, lowering the number of victims substantially.

After all the flames were completely extinguished and it was safe to enter the mine, workers were thrilled to find that eight of the work mules located on slope no. 1 were somehow still alive (along with a small kitten).

The cause of the fire was never fully determined. The disaster made nine widows and twenty-one orphans that tragic day.

The men killed were Aaron Isaacson (age twenty-six), Otis Newhouse (age thirty-eight), John E. Jones (age twenty), Carl Berger (age forty-eight), William Arundale (age forty), James Gurrell (age fifty), Ben Hardy (age sixty), Dominick Bartolera (age forty-five), Aaron Isaacson (age thirty) and Tom Marsolich (age thirty). The bodies of two workers, Philip Pozarich (age thirty-one) and George Tomach (age unknown), were never retrieved. Rescuers got as close as a few hundred yards from their bodies, but dangerous conditions and falling timbers forced them to pull back. All the men except Newhouse and Gurrell were buried at the expense of the Miners Union at the cemetery in Roslyn. Rest in peace.

Do the spirits of these brave, hardworking men roam the cemetery late at night, still in shock? Some think so.

Note: For a more detailed look at the dangerous world of mining, read "Underground Coal Mine Disasters 1900–2010: Events, Responses, and a Look to the Future." This paper captures almost 110 years of history of underground coal mine disasters in the United States and is available at: https://www.cdc.gov/niosh/mining/UserFiles/works/pdfs/ucmdn.pdf.

RITZVILLE

When the Northern Pacific Railroad established a station in the town in 1881, Ritzville soon became a legitimate stop for travelers. It was named after Philip Ritz (1827–1889, age sixty-one), an early settler who was responsible for grading ten miles of the railroad bed. Soon, eager wheat farmers arrived. These farmers mostly came to Ritzville from South Dakota. At one time, Ritz owned a whopping ten thousand acres in the state of Washington, much of it along proposed railroad routes, including parts of Seattle and Tacoma.

Ritzville had very desirable land perfect for wheat farming, and when the word got out, men traveled from as far as Germany to establish their land claims.

Today, almost two thousand people call Ritzville their home.

RITZVILLE CARNEGIE LIBRARY

The Ritzville Carnegie Library is on the National Register of Historic Places—and has its very own resident ghost!

Local Daniel Buchanan created a small library in 1902 when he donated 268 books to the town, which were housed in a space above a store. In 1903, the town allocated $1,000 toward the maintenance of the library. By 1906, the citizens of Ritzville had convinced the very wealthy Andrew

The Ritzville Carnegie Library, built in 1907, is haunted by a former librarian named Ida. *Courtesy of LOC#2018699114, Carol M. Highsmith, photographer.*

Carnegie to help, and he pledged $10,000 toward a permanent library if the town secured and maintained a location for it. At that time, Ritzville was the smallest town in the United States to receive financial assistance from Carnegie for a library. The town was lucky enough to secure an architectural firm from Spokane, Preusse & Zittel, to draw up the plans. The building ended up costing $10,500 to construct in 1907. It still operates today as Ritzville's library.

Some claim that the ghost of Ida, a former librarian, haunts the building. Who was Ida? Why does she haunt the library? Could the ghost possibly be the spirit of someone else, perhaps a local who loved to while away the hours casually reading a favorite book?

NOTE: The Ritzville Carnegie Library building is located at 302 West Main Avenue, Ritzville, Washington 99169.

STEPTOE BUTTE

Steptoe Butte, in Whitman County, occupies a particular place in Washington's history. Some people see orbs and strange lights above the butte. Perhaps it is something unusual; perhaps it is just a weather anomaly…

Steptoe Butte in 1910, with the Cashup Hotel in the distance. On March 11, 1911, the hotel caught fire, caused by two boys who were smoking. *Courtesy of Steve Shook via Wikipedia.*

Steptoe Butte holds the spirit of James S. "Cashup" Davis (1815–1896, age eighty) who was a local icon and loved by both tourists and Steptoe citizens. No story about Steptoe Butte would be complete without adding the fascinating history of Davis and his beautiful hotel.

Davis was born in 1815 in Hastings, England. After some bouncing around, he wound up on a passenger ship heading to New York City in 1840. He made his way to Ohio, where he fell in love with Mary Ann Shoemaker (1827–1894, age sixty-seven), and they got married in 1844. Together, they had twelve children.

The year 1860 found the Davis family in Wisconsin, and by 1870, they were living in Iowa. About 1872, the Davis family moved to the Steptoe area.

In 1888, Davis built the Cashup Davis Hotel and Summer Resort, nestled at the very top of the butte, for $10,000. Davis had earned his nickname because whenever his customers offered to buy something he would tell them they would have to "cash up" the money—because (like the smart man he was) he refused to give credit.

The railroad soon came through Steptoe Butte, and Davis jumped on the opportunity to expand his business adventures. He built a road that cost him $1,400, a beautiful stage, a sixty-six-by-sixty-six-foot building, a house, a barn, horse corrals and a stagecoach stop designed to delight weary travelers going back and forth from Walla Walla to Spokane. He also built a general store with a very lucrative dance hall upstairs—to keep everyone entertained as people danced the polka and the waltz.

Davis added a dining room that could easily feed fifty hungry people. On top of the hotel, he constructed a large cupola where people could enjoy viewing the expanse of the hills or simply read a book while relaxing. The surprising addition of a telescope became a favorite, allowing people to magically see over one hundred miles in the distance.

The hotel was the oldest landmark in Eastern Washington at its peak and treasured by everyone who visited.

Davis's health slowly declined, and he spent more and more time alone in the hotel parlor with his beloved dog. The hotel was also declining, and visitors were far and few between, adding to his worries. In 1896, Davis passed away in his favorite parlor in the hotel with his loving canine by his side. His funeral procession consisted of many horse-drawn carriages as he was well-known and well-respected in town.

The hotel was vacant for a number of years. But on March 11, 1911, just before sunset, the hotel tragically caught fire, and the flames quickly spread. (Later, it was discovered that the fire was caused by two mischievous teenagers smoking cigarettes.) Travelers could see the blazing red-hot flames shooting into the air from miles away.

Before Davis died, he said he wished to be buried on the butte, but unfortunately, the rock was too hard to blast through to dig him a proper grave. Extremely heavy rainfall the day of his death (oddly, over twenty-nine inches of rain is marked on his funeral expense bill) also contributed to the change of burial plans. Instead, he was buried at the base of the butte in the Bethel Cemetery.

COLFAX

The early history of Colfax is a fascinating tale of early pioneers, mills and growth. The area that would become Colfax was once home to bands of Palouse and the Nez Perce tribe. In the summer of 1870, James Perkins (1842–1920, age seventy-nine) and Thomas Smith arrived in the area. They claimed land at the north and south branches of the Palouse River on July 10, 1870. Initially, Perkins called his tiny settlement Belleville. However, he

The beautiful Colfax City Hall and Colfax Fire Department building, constructed in 1913. *Courtesy of LOC #2017790261, Russell Lee, photographer.*

later changed the name to Colfax in honor of Schuyler Colfax (vice president to President Ulysses S. Grant).

Soon, other settlers came to the area to lay down roots. In 1872, platting of the land began, and the town started taking shape. Colfax was incorporated on January 14, 1879, and William H. James was elected as its first mayor. A sawmill was built to supply wood to meet the newcomers' demands, but progress was slow and trees were hard to come by. Soon after the mill began operating, log drives along the Palouse River commenced. Colfax grew into a prosperous town, serving as a nexus of services for wheat growers throughout the region.

Today, almost three thousand people are proud to call Colfax their home. But behind the interesting layers of Colfax's history, there lies a darker, more sinister and eerie side.

ST. IGNATIUS HOSPITAL

Constructed in the 1890s by the Sisters of Charity nuns, led by Mother Joseph Pariseau, St. Ignatius Hospital operated as a medical facility from 1893 to 1964. In 1968, it became the St. Ignatius Manor, a residence for those needing assisted living and those considered mentally insane. It is rumored that a patient once "fell" out of a third-floor window, adding to the long list of people who died at the site.

On a square plaque outside of St. Ignatius Hospital, a Latin inscription reads, "CHARITAS CHRISTI URGET NOS," or "The love of Christ impels us."

The historic building continues to entice and excite people of all ages, as it is a known paranormal hot spot. The mysterious ghost of a woman dressed in 1920s attire roams the mezzanine of St. Ignatius Hospital. Perhaps she was a patient, a nurse or someone with unfinished business to attend to? Her footsteps echo in the dusty hallways and within the walls of peeling paint. Reports of visitors hearing strange growls and being attacked by unseen hands are all too common. St. Ignatius Hospital is so full of mysterious characters from its past that it is hard to condense their stories down to a few pages.

In 1918, the influenza epidemic infected roughly 500 million people—one third of the world's population—and caused 50 million deaths worldwide.

St. Ignatius Hospital offers ghosts tours while it's being renovated. The building has several mysterious spirits and appeared on *Ghost Adventures* and *Ghost Hunters*. *Public domain postcard, 1900 unknown author, courtesy of Wikipedia.*

In the United States, a quarter of the population caught the virus, and an incredible 675,000 died.

At St. Ignatius Hospital, thousands of children and adults succumbed to flu and died within its walls. Many think these souls linger at the old hospital, confused, tortured and unable to move on. Whispers of the past intertwine with the present, revealing spectral tales as mysterious as they are fascinating.

This reportedly haunted hospital gained so much national attention that it landed an episode of the popular show *Ghost Adventures* (season 21, episode 2) with Zak Bagans and his crew, after they personally investigated the building. The TAPS team from *Ghost Hunters* also conducted a very productive investigation during which they researched and physically explored the hospital (season 16, episode 6).

People witness a shadow person who has "overly large hands" on the third floor of the hospital. Though the entity seems larger than life, he is not an aggressive or angry spirit. Instead, he just seems trapped in time.

Many believe this ghost is E.F. Martin (1858–1893, age thirty-five), the first person to ever die within the walls of the brand-new hospital, in 1893. Martin was a brakeman for the Union Pacific Railroad. He was an efficient and hardworking man who was known for getting the job done.

Martin was a big man with strong, broad shoulders and very large hands. On June 23, he was coupling two railroad cars near the Colfax train depot. One of the cars was an older model (part of the Sanger & Lent's Circus Train) and Martin was not experienced in handling it. He struggled with inserting the pin to connect the two cars. Unfortunately, he couldn't get the pin inserted in time, allowing the cars to come together, crushing him in between. One car jolted back, and he was tossed aside near the tracks. Doctor Boswell hurried to the man's aid, and Martin was rushed off to St. Ignatius Hospital. He died from his injuries at ten thirty that night. His body was examined in the basement morgue, then buried at the city cemetery. It is very likely that Martin is the large-handed ghost often seen on the third floor of the hospital.

Room 312 once housed an angry disabled man named Michael. He was bound to a wheelchair and died in his room at the hospital. He continues to haunt his old room and is considered mean and evil. His spirit has a bad temper and tends to viciously grab people. Sometimes a large amount of flies swarms inside his room.

Another true-life patient was a woman named Rose who lived in room 311 during the 1970s when the hospital was used as an assisted living facility. Her spirit is also angry, and people have seen bizarre shadow figures and heard ghostly moans, strange growling and other eerie sounds inside her old room.

The former operating room is a highly active paranormal hot spot. People have reported extremely cold (almost freezing) temperatures and even the feeling of being "hugged" by frozen arms! Others have reported feelings of nausea and stomach pains when inside the walls of the old operating room. One female entity whispered, "I'm stuck in the crypt"—as recorded on the *Ghost Adventures* crew's equipment!

Some of the ghosts that walk the halls of St. Ignatius Hospital are phantom nurses. These spirits move up and down the hallways in an authoritative manner. Perhaps they are still attending to patients and administering medications, as they are heard moving in and out of various rooms?

Some suggest the paranormal specters are the spirits of two young nurses who contracted the Spanish flu and died at the very hospital where they were working to help others. Irene Ellwart (1898–1918, age twenty) was just a young woman when she succumbed to influenza. She was born in St. John, Washington, to A.J. Ellwart from Russia and Josephine from Illinois. Dedicated to her patients, she tended to Mrs. Frank Hanna right up until the day she died. Tragically, poor Irene would die just a few days later from the same flu that killed Mrs. Hanna and be buried in the Colfax Cemetery. Her young heart had yet to experience so much in life as she fell victim to pneumonia complicated by influenza.

Her coworker Gertrude Mary Fuchs (1896–1918, age twenty-two) had also been a nurse for the past two years at St. Ignatius. Born to Paul Fuchs from Germany and Mary Hageman from Illinois, she too would succumb to the same fate as Irene. Just a week after she contacted the Spanish flu, her parents were making funeral arrangements for their young daughter. Gertrude would be laid to rest at St. Boniface Catholic Cemetery. Both girls died at St. Ignatius, devoting themselves to helping others right up until their deaths.

Still other ghosts are seen within the walls of the vacant hospital: phantom children running and playing and several watchful nuns. Some believe they are ghostly remnants of the Sisters of Charity, who once cared for the sick there and may still watch over their beloved hospital.

The Colfax Chamber of Commerce used to offer tours and ghost hunts at the hospital to try to generate income for the small town. Unfortunately, the building's resident ghosts scared away anyone who was willing to give the tours! The moneymaking idea quickly came to a halt.

The new owners, Austin and Laura Storm, purchased this historic site in the spring of 2021 with the vision of breathing life back into its timeworn walls. The Storms aim to restore St. Ignatius into a potential hotel, with studio spaces or artist rooms. While the Storms work on structural improvements, they continue to offer haunted tours of the hospital. Ghost enthusiasts can explore the halls, seeking spectral encounters.

NOTE: Once the structure is secure, the Storms look forward to the exciting phase of window restoration and further fleshing out the hospital's spaces. If you're curious or intrigued, you can sign up for their haunted tours and ghost hunts or follow their progress on Instagram at @stignatiuscolfax. St. Ignatius is located at 1009 South Mill Street, Colfax, Washington 99111.

THE GHOST OF AGNES DOWNS

Inside the walls of St. Ignatius Hospital is the restless spirit of Agnes Downs (1881–1904, age twenty-three), who suffered a heartbreaking death at a young age. The scandal that revolved around her delicate condition shocked the small community and led to one of the biggest, most disputed manslaughter cases of the year.

Agnes was born near Astoria, Oregon, to Don Alphonso Downs (1854–1912, age fifty-eight) and Lavina Elizabeth Dollarhide (1853–1904, age fifty-one). The Downs family moved to Whitman around 1887 when Agnes was just six years old. Not much is known about her until she began studying to become a teacher at Pullman in 1900. There she fell in love with her professor of modern languages, Edwin A. Snow. Elegant man that he was, he was also actively involved in the glee club and appeared as a pianist in a local performance of the operetta *Alesia*.

Agnes graduated from Washington Agricultural College with her class of 1903 and soon became a teacher herself. But she would soon find herself in trouble with an unexpected and unwanted pregnancy.

Agnes claimed that while living in room 43 at Hotel Whitman, she had become intimately involved with a man named Raymond Morris Austin (also called Dr. Charles Auston, a dentist). Their affair lasted for only a few weeks. Agnes soon found herself in a bit of a bind: she discovered she was pregnant. On March 21, she decided to tell Raymond about her condition. They had been seeing each other for only forty-three days.

bonds. The case is attracting the widest attention and the court room is daily thronged with curious spectators. On account of the high social status of all the parties concerned the keenest interest is evidenced in even the most conservative circles and the outcome of the case is awaited with much anxiety.

SOCIAL   mmm

Mrs. Frank Allyn and Mrs. Turner will entertain at cards tomorrow, at the home of the former.

SPOKANE LEAVES
FOR ALASKA PORTS

DR. T. D. FERGUSON.

Agnes Downs, Dr. Ferguson and Professor Edwin Snow were all entangled in the trial of the century after Agnes died from an illegal abortion. *Courtesy of the* Seattle Star, *June 24, 1904.*

"Go to Doctor Ferguson, and he will relieve you of your condition," Austin told her. The frightened young woman went to see Dr. Ferguson, who quietly prescribed medicines that would secretly terminate the pregnancy. But they did not work.

On March 31, eight days later, Agnes tentatively went to see the doctor again at his office in Colfax.

"Austin will pay the fifty dollars for the services," she told him.

(On her deathbed, Agnes confessed to being intimate with Snow and claimed that he was the father of her baby. Were there really several other loves in Miss Downs's life? Or was she protecting the identity of her one lover by inventing other paramours? If so, why?)

Apparently, this is where all the stories from all the people involved get tricky. During the trials to come, many conflicting versions of the incident would surface.

In order to understand the dreadful circumstances that ultimately took Agnes's life, one must evaluate all the evidence—and why she may continue to haunt the hospital where she died. At that time, she was already fragile and emotionally unstable, as her mother, Lavina, had just died on April 17.

Agnes had been temporarily living in the nearby Barry household off and on for years. She disclosed her situation to Mrs. Barry, who informed a family physician, Dr. Russel. After examining Agnes, Dr. Russell suggested the abortion should be performed at the nearby Scott home to keep her condition a secret. (In the early 1900s, becoming pregnant out of wedlock was a social catastrophe. Abortion was completely illegal; in a few states, it would not be legalized until the late 1960s. Dr. Ferguson disagreed. He demanded Agnes go to St. Ignatius Hospital.

"If she should die here [at the Barry house], there might be court inquiry, and we do not want that," Ferguson said. He also desired to keep her condition secret from the world.

Another physician from Spokane, Dr. Essig, also examined Agnes. He, too, felt she should move to St. Ignatius for monitoring. "I would not attempt to cover up one crime by committing another!" he yelled.

Eventually, Agnes would be moved to the hospital, where her condition rapidly deteriorated. Her brother, Don Ray Downs, tried in vain to get other doctors to tend to her, as he felt she was not getting the care she needed to survive the ordeal. But Dr. Ferguson refused to allow anyone else to help Agnes. Why?

Finally, Agnes made a deathbed statement in front of her brother and a Dr. J.F. Hall. (Interestingly, it was reported that Dr. Hall was also "in a criminal, intimate relationship" with Agnes two years before her death.)

She began her statement by saying, "I, Agnes R. Downs, feeling under the solemn sense of impending death do hereby make the following declaration as to the cause of my present condition…" Then she spoke of her brief affair with Austin, described how the illegal abortion was done at Dr. Ferguson's office and stated the procedure was effectual. "Dr. Ferguson, previous to March 31, 1904, gave me lots of medicine to cause an unlawful operation, which failed. Dated this 20th day of April 1904, 11:15 p.m." The defense went to great lengths to disallow this deathbed statement to be introduced, but Judge Neterer finally permitted it as evidence.

When Dr. Ferguson went to the witness stand, he told a whole different version of the story. "Agnes told me that she herself had committed the crime (abortion) before I was even called to attend to her," he told the jury. He also claimed he treated her for fake "appendicitis" to cover up her sin.

Dr. Hall told the jury that Agnes had contracted blood poisoning "caused by a procedure performed by a sharp instrument" and that the poisoning was what caused her death. It was also discovered later that Hall had procured Agnes's deathbed statement about Austin "in the hopes of making the young man responsible for Miss Downs' condition." So was Dr. Hall still intimate with Agnes before she died? If not, what was he trying to cover up? And why?

As Agnes grew weaker and weaker, she called for the Sisters to be by her side and pray for her. On April 21, Agnes took her final breath.

Doctor Wilson Johnston of Colfax performed the postmortem examination and determined undeniably that an "unlawful operation had been performed on Agnes."

Sheriff Canull arrested Dr. Ferguson on May 10, 1904. He was formally charged with manslaughter for performing an illegal abortion. The police would go after Snow and Austin as well, as accomplices in her demise. (At one point, Agnes had said that Snow actually performed the abortion.)

But Snow was no dummy, and three days before Ferguson got arrested, he severed his connection with the college, resigned and promptly left town—leaving the picture forever.

The trial dragged on and on. Over twelve other doctors came to Ferguson's aid, explaining things away in technical, confusing medical jargon. It seemed as though not taking any responsibility for the illegal procedure that was performed was the most important thing. Did they want Agnes silenced after the abortion was botched, so they refused to treat her? Was the only way to secure their continued positions as physicians to let her die? They certainly did not want to risk losing their licenses to practice medicine over a silly young sexually promiscuous girl.

There are many unanswered questions and oddities in this entire story. Things just don't add up.

The Whitman County Courthouse where Dr. Ferguson was tried for the manslaughter of Agnes Downs in 1904. *Courtesy of SPL, #4625.*

The jurors deliberated for seven long, grueling hours. In the end, they decided Dr. Ferguson was not guilty of manslaughter. The jury simply could not determine whether Agnes had tried to abort the unwanted pregnancy herself or with the help of others.

Dr. T. Dinsmore Ferguson died at his home in Colfax in early October 1908 of heart disease after being ill for three months.

Many believe the angry ghost that haunts St. Ignatius Hospital is the tragic spirit of Agnes Downs. She was a beautiful young woman who lived passionately and was a victim—not just of a botched abortion, but also of the rules and expectations of the difficult era for women in which she lived.

BLOODY SHIRTS BY THE RIVER

The day started off like any other for Colfax local E.K. Loyd. But as he was walking along the bank of the Palouse River, the disturbing sight of several bloody white shirts caught his attention. As he inspected them, he discovered that he had stumbled upon evidence of foul play.

Loyd nervously made his way to town and told Deputy Sheriff Matlock about the scene. The two men returned to the river together, where Matlock investigated Loyd's findings. One shirt had five stab-type bloody cuts in it—typical of marks made by a knife. The others had blood on them as well, but the river had muddied them up. Matlock found a small diary in one of the pockets. He also unfolded two banknote slips, each from the Banco de Occident of Mexico, dated May 2, 1892 (six years before Matlock found them) for deposits made out to John Schiess, $600 each (about $45,000 today).

Loyd and Matlock also found a deed transfer written in Spanish to one Juan Rubin of Guatemala. In another pocket was a certification from a court clerk at Multnomah County, Oregon: papers for becoming a United States citizen, signed by W.H. Harris on September 14, 1892. (It is not known who exactly Juan Rubin was.)

Another bloody shirt told the definitive story of a struggle. A lot of blood had accumulated around the neck area, possibly from a knife slash. A wallet was found inside a flour sack; its contents were not disclosed to the public.

Matlock gathered the evidence and returned to the station. No body was to be seen anywhere near where the bloody shirts had been found.

Curious, Matlock went back out to Loyd's rented farm and racetrack near the fairgrounds. Oddly, the owner of the property was none other than the murdered man: John Schiess.

Did Loyd kill Schiess? Was there some sort of disgruntlement between the men? If Loyd killed Schiess, why would he disclose the bloody shirts to Matlock instead of burning or burying them? Did Loyd toss Schiess's body in the Palouse River, only for the current to pull the shirts from it and deposit them on the muddy bank? If so, where was Schiess's body? Since the farm Loyd lived on was also a racetrack, did the men have a disagreement over a gambling debt, perhaps? Schiess appeared to have a substantial amount of money in his bank account; was money the motive for the murder?

No further records of Schiess's disappearance have been found, and his body was never recovered. His untimely death is forgotten in history: a victim of foul play, another tragic tale of greed and gain gone wrong.

If you spot the ghostly apparition of a man covered in blood near the Palouse River, it is most likely the angry spirit of John Schiess.

NOTE: Research shows a Mr. John Schiess homesteaded eighty acres of land on May 20, 1862, in Willamette, Oregon. This might be the same man, because a John Schiess had also applied for citizenship papers in Multnomah County near Portland, Oregon, about twenty miles away from Willamette.

COLFAX UFO INCIDENT

Washington state has a rich history of UFO sightings, and Colfax has played its part in this cosmic intrigue. There have been so many sightings in the state that it's earned the nickname UFO Capital of the Nation.

Since 1946, Washington residents have reported a whopping 148,454 sightings, 7,812 of which the National UFO Reporting Center (https://nuforc.org) has filtered and listed as legitimate in its online database. Interestingly, the National UFO Reporting Center itself is based in Washington. Located inside a decommissioned U.S. Air Force missile base between Davenport and Harrington in Lincoln County, it serves as a hub for UFO enthusiasts and investigators.

Washington's UFO legacy stretches back to the days when Boise pilot Kenneth Arnold spotted nine large, shiny objects flying near Mount Rainier. (See "Mount Rainier UFOs" on page 22.)

Official Salem, Massachusetts coast guard photo identification no. 5554 (1952) that shows unidentified flying objects flying in a *V* pattern. *Courtesy of LOC # 2007680837, Shell Alpert, photographer.*

Many people believe we are not alone in this world and aliens visit our planet regularly. Others think aliens are currently living among us, even side by side, virtually undetected. Others still believe that paranormal activity is caused by aliens, not by ghosts.

One such incident in Colfax captured the attention of countless citizens. In 1950, multiple residents reported a series of UFO sightings over the course of several nights. Witnesses described seeing unusual lights and strange, unfamiliar objects in the sky, which soon attracted the attention of the media, both newspapers and radio stations. The movements of the objects were unlike anything locals had seen before. They were moving erratically and performing maneuvers that were beyond the capabilities of any known aircraft at the time.

Shortly before midnight on Saturday, July 19, 1952, at Washington National Airport, air traffic controller Edward Nugent spotted seven slow-moving objects on his radar screen. These mysterious blips appeared far from any known civilian or military flight paths. He jokingly referred to them as a "fleet of flying saucers."

Following the UFO sightings, the U.S. Air Force Project Blue Book team investigated the reports and determined that natural phenomena or misidentifications were behind these sightings. Between the years 1953 and 1958, the Air Force logged an incredible 20,764 reports of UFOs. When they were asked how many of the 20,764 they'd identified as aircraft known to them, they answered only 2.2 percent—but continued to deny any knowledge of UFOs' existence. So the Air Force could not explain what 97.8 percent of the confirmed UFO reports filed in five years were?

CHAPTER 3
LOWER EASTERN REGION

YAKIMA TO WALLA WALLA TO PULLMAN
AND THEN SOME

YAKIMA

*Well, you may say there are no such things as spooks, but when you put
your hand out and it isn't there, that settles it.*
—*Unknown boy who saw the woman in black in 1897 and reported it*
to the Yakima Herald

Beer lovers can thank the wonderful, fertile soil in the Yakima Valley for supplying the most crucial factor in beer production: hops. Yakima farms produce a whopping 80 percent of the United States' hop crops. Weather is a crucial factor for hop crops, and the Yakima Valley's rich volcanic soil, Cascade mountain water and long, sun-filled days all contribute to prime growing conditions.

The city of Yakima occupies what was once the traditional hunting and gathering grounds of the region's tribes, known collectively as the Peoples of the Plateau. They enjoyed fishing for the local, abundant salmon and steelhead that kept their bellies full. The first White settlers were cattle ranchers.

Over the years, the farms have served their owners well and now also provide acres of bountiful grapes for vineyards. Yakima County yields over nineteen thousand acres of grapes, keeping wine drinkers happy.

But Yakima has a more sinister side. Several haunted places keep the city of Yakima even more interesting.

Ghosts in Yakima have been reported as far back as 1897. This postcard depicts Yakima Avenue in 1907. *Courtesy of SPL, #5658.*

THE WOMAN IN BLACK

Dating as far back as 1897, persistent rumors of an aggressive female ghost near Naches Avenue in North Yakima have been reported by locals. The spirit was first seen the night of a social gathering at the home of a Miss Meyer. The spirit was described as a tall, thin woman dressed entirely in black who floated effortlessly, making no sound. The ghost was so scary that one of Miss Meyer's guests, Miss Zenovia Fulkerson, ran from the estate screaming out into the street.

The apparition makes absolutely no noise as she glides effortlessly around the streets of North Yakima. She has been seen for over 150 years by many witnesses. Some claim she approaches them, almost rushes up to them, then expels a deep, hissing breath onto them. She has been known to reach out to people, but if they are brave enough to try to touch her, she evaporates into thin air.

One frosty night, local men Edgar Gunn and Arthur Englehart were walking down the street chatting when they noticed a woman sitting on the stoop of the Presbyterian church across the street. They worried that the young woman might be in distress. Just as soon as they thought this, the ghost stood up and quickly glided over to them. Astonished, the men froze in their tracks. When the spirit got close to them, it reached out as if to touch their

A tall, slender female ghost dressed in a long black dress has haunted Yakima for over 150 years and been seen by many witnesses. *Courtesy of LOC #2010716159, Charles Dana Gibson, artist, 1901.*

faces. Suddenly, it let out a high-pitched screech, then instantly disappeared. The two men were shocked and had no idea what had just happened.

Another time, the ghost was seen on Naches Avenue in town by a couple of young boys. As they followed the spirit, quick on her heels, they witnessed her mysteriously moving "through" the foundation of Mike Schorn's home, as if the foundation was not solid matter.

Officer Grant was quickly called to the scene to investigate. Armed with a lantern (remember, this was 1897), Grant slowly descended into the basement of the Schorn home. He made a thorough search but never located the mysterious woman in black.

A few months later, Ms. Barbara Jackson saw the ghost and reported it. Mrs. William Lewis was next to witness the ghost. A few days later, George Steinweg looked out his window and noticed his horse running frantically around its pasture. The woman in black was chasing his horse!

Another dark night, Irvy Bounds and Max Bogle were walking along a bridge when they saw the restless spirit. Curious, they moved closer. She seemed to stare at them as they approached her. When the boys got close enough, she reached out to them. Startled, the boys froze. She quickly shoved Bogle so hard that the buttons of his coat were torn off.

Who is this strange female ghost that haunts the streets? There may be some historical facts that support the story of the mysterious woman in black who has plagued North Yakima for so long.

In January 1890, a lovely courtesan named Jennie White (1866–1890, age twenty-four) lived in the North Yakima area. She feared her secret lover was going to leave her, so instead of suffering from heartbreak, she overdosed on morphine, quickly ending her life. Could poor Jennie be the restless spirit who continues to roam the street searching for her lover?

While alive, Jennie also went by the names Mamie Stetson and Maud Stetson, and she tried to keep a low profile. Although she worked as a lady of the night, she was madly in love with a man named S.M. Gumbrents. (No record of an S.M. Gumbrents can be found, so he may have been using an alias, too.)

After some relationship difficulties and personal struggles, Jennie decided to end it all. One lonely night at a nearby lodging house, Jennie would write her final farewell letter:

S.M. Gumbrents, The key is under some paper under the bureau drawer. Good night. From your dear friend, Mamie Stetson.

At ten thirty the next morning, concerned about her fragile lodger, the landlady checked in on Jennie, only to discover her dead body. The key she had written about was the key to her trunk, which sat near the bed. Jennie was originally from San Francisco, California, and had relatives in Portland, Oregon. Her lifeless body was taken by Bonney & Stewart Undertaking.

Tragic stories like Jennie's are all too common. Hers was one of the countless deaths barely mentioned in the newspapers; just a few simple blurbs were written about the tragic event.

If Jennie is truly the heartbroken ghost who wanders the streets of North Yakima, it would be no wonder. Perhaps she is still searching for her lover, Mr. Gumbrents.

CAPITOL THEATRE

The Capitol Theatre is home to a very friendly ghost. It is currently a performing arts venue: the stage is home to productions by many local organizations, such as the Yakima Symphony Orchestra and Town Hall and community concerts, as well as traveling Broadway musicals.

The original theater was designed by B. Marcus Priteca and was the brainstorm of Frederick Mercy Sr. (1877–1937, age sixty). Mercy was from San Francisco, California, and came to Yakima Valley in 1912 with his wife, Beryl, and three sons: Frederick Jr., Edgar and Paul. It opened its grand doors to the public on April 5, 1920, as the Mercy Theatre, named after its owner. It was the largest theater in the Pacific Northwest at the time and featured exciting vaudeville acts to entertain both locals and travelers. The smash hit that year was *Maytime*, and every one of the theater's two thousand seats was full for the performance.

The theater was added to the National Register of Historic Places on April 11, 1973. Yet after its ownership was transferred to the city, the theater was severely damaged by a fire on August 11, 1975; only the walls of the audience section remained standing. One of the few items saved from the fire was a Steinway grand piano (signed by Henry E. Steinway, the president of Steinway, himself) and the stage-house (the backstage area where sets, props and technical equipment are stored and from which actors enter and exit the stage during performances).

The theater was painstakingly rebuilt and once again was the highlight of the town.

The Capitol Theatre in Yakima is haunted by a friendly ghost named Shorty, who was a technician at the theater and hanged himself over lost love. *Courtesy Cacophony 2007, via Wikimedia Commons.*

The Capitol Theatre is said to be haunted by a ghost possibly named Shorty Michaud, who was a technician at the theater. After being rejected by a beautiful actress, Shorty tragically took his own life, hanging himself above the stage sometime in the 1930s. Reports of Shorty's ghostly presence include inexplicable noises, frigid hallways, blasts of freezing cold air, bizarre balls of light and a strange voice calling out people's names. Employees even claim the toilets flush by themselves when they are cleaning the bathrooms.

No one really knows why Shorty continues to haunt the building. Or Perhaps Mr. Mercy himself still roams the beautiful theater he loved so much when he was alive?

NOTE: The Capitol Theatre is located at 19 South Third Street, Yakima, Washington 98901. For a more complete outline of the incredible history of the Capitol Theatre, visit: https://capitoltheatre.org/about.

THE DEPOT RESTAURANT

One of the most haunted locations in Yakima is the old Depot Restaurant on North Front Street. Some claim the building is occupied by up to seven spirits! Built in 1910, it was once a Northern Pacific Railway stop. But the building also served a more eerie purpose: it was a loading zone for the dead.

A seriously devastating epidemic of typhoid fever raged through Yakima in the early 1910s, with a death rate five times higher than the national average, killing many locals. In order to keep up with the rapidly decomposing victims, the furnace in the station was used as a makeshift crematory. During those early years, typhoid fever was responsible for almost 30 percent of recorded deaths. Could the spirits of the cremated be haunting the station?

Once a bountiful restaurant and lounge, the building is now closed up, ready for its next adventure.

The ghosts in the station are said to be active regularly. Some have seen and heard the spirits of young children roaming the rooms, laughing and playing. Organ music has been heard playing mysteriously when no organ is being used or even located on the site. Who is playing the strange music and why? Objects moving by themselves, cold spots, unexplained odors and noises are all just everyday occurrences people have experienced at the old building.

The old depot building on North Front Street has multiple ghosts. Shown here is the Northern Pacific Depot and Park at North Yakima in 1900. *Courtesy of SPL #4742.*

One of the more notorious ghosts is a beautiful female entity whose apparition has been seen wearing a white apron with her hair pulled up in a bun. Who is she? Her identity has never been revealed. Was she an employee of the railway? Or was she possibly a helpful nurse caring for those in need during the epidemic?

NOTE: The old Depot Restaurant building is located at 32 North Front Street in Yakima, Washington 98901.

THE GHOST OF LADY LUND

The ghost of Lady Lund, wife of the original proprietor, haunts the old brick Lund Building, gliding effortlessly around the rooms to this day.

In 1893, Thomas Proctor Lund (1855–1906, age fifty) purchased the Morrison lot for $3,000 in hopes of creating a unique space. A few years later, in 1899, Thomas erected the Lund Building with the help of architect Charles Bruenn and contractor A.F. Switzer. To the tune of $4,000, they completed what was called the Alfalfa Saloon, where he also served as the proprietor. The saloon was located within the Lund Building at the northeast corner of Front Street and Yakima Avenue near the Northern Pacific depot, which operated until 1910, when it became the Chicago Clothing Company (until 1968).

Thomas Lund was born in Norway. He came to the United States with big plans. He married Emma Belle (1861–1944, age eighty-two) in 1887, and the couple was happily married for eighteen years.

In 1899, a man named Joe Ponti took over the Alfalfa Saloon. In 1905, Thomas was again in charge of the Alfalfa and took to remodeling the building, creating updated spaces for lodging upstairs. In 1908, Ernest Lund (Thomas's son) became the new proprietor.

Thomas died unexpectedly on January 10, 1906, of "rheumatism of the heart." Emma remarried a few times and lived to the ripe old age of eighty-two.

For twenty-five years, the building held the incredible Greystone Restaurant, filling the bellies of tourists and locals alike (it's now closed). Patrons and employees of the Greystone saw Lady Lund floating effortlessly across the floor. She appeared without feet; her apparition had long hair and wore a long, flowing dress. Former Greystone owner Mark Strosahl (1952–2010, age fifty-eight) saw Lady Lund in his restaurant many times.

She would frequently photobomb people when they were taking pictures in the foyer. When the pictures were viewed, in place of the person being photographed stood a hazy female figure wearing a long dress!

The sounds of high heels walking around is often heard—when no one is wearing high heels…

Why does Lady Lund hang around her former husband's building? Is she simply watching over things? No one really knows her motive for haunting the building, but she sure has a good time doing it.

NOTE: The 5,200-square-foot, multistory brick Lund Building is located at 5 North Front Street in downtown Yakima and has played host to many different businesses over the years. It is the oldest surviving structure in the district.

THE YAKIMA SPORTS CENTER

The building known as the Yakima Sports Center has been known to be haunted by a ghost (or two) over the years. It remains a historic icon in the city and has been transformed into many things since it was built.

It was built by Fred Schaefer (1870–1953, age eighty-three), who became a local proprietor in Yakima.

Schaefer, who was born in Illinois and eventually found his way to Yakima in 1905, had a keen interest in the theater business. In 1908, he constructed his Schaefer Theater in East Yakima and soon became a local favorite, entertaining many with various plays. The well-known Valley Inn was housed on the second floor.

In 1911, Schaefer wished to move his theater from East Yakima to the blossoming West Yakima area, so he tried to secure a lease in the Davis Building. Later, in 1917, the building became the Columbia Hotel & Diner, with card tables and an eating area that operated successfully for decades.

During the COVID-19 pandemic, the restaurant suffered and temporarily closed. Now reopened, the Sports Center offers live music and entertainment, great brews, pool tables, fun events and Gus's Pizza (part of the Sports Center, an Italian restaurant known for its casual atmosphere, cocktails, coffee, comfort food and late-night offerings).

Over the years, many employees have experienced strange phenomena in the building. Is it possible that residual energy remains from when the building was used for sinful pleasures during the Prohibition—profitable

The Yakima Sports Center is haunted by the American writer Raymond Carver, who grew up in Yakima and often returned to visit. *Courtesy of the* Peninsula Daily News, *1988.*

brothels, illegal drinking and the many hazards of bootlegging? The sounds of glasses clinking as if in celebration, disembodied voices, phantom footsteps and smokey apparitions have been seen and heard by many.

Some believe the resident ghost is that of American short story writer and poet Raymond Carver (1938–1988, age fifty). Born into a hardworking middle-class family, Carver knew how difficult life can be and brought this understanding forth into his poems and stories. He published his first collection of stories in 1976, and in 1981, he received immediate acclaim for his breakout collection titled *What We Talk About When We Talk About Love*, which established him as an important figure in the literary world. Carver grew up in Yakima but bounced around most of the rest of his life. He suffered from a heavy drinking problem, and although he was deemed financially and professionally successful by many, that was not enough for him. But a few failed marriages and broken relationships later, Carver was finally able to conquer his alcoholism.

Is it possible that Carter returned to his hometown after his passing? Some spirits are known to return to a simpler, happier time in their lives or a place they loved and enjoyed when they were alive.

Is the friendly male entity that bounces around the Sports Center really Carver? Maybe it is the great atmosphere, fun people and ever-flowing booze that keeps the old, hard-drinking Carver interested. Visit and enjoy a cold beer and a great pizza, and perhaps the ghost of Carver will come sit by you and keep you company.

NOTE: The Yakima Sports Center is located at 214 East Yakima Avenue, Yakima, Washington 98901.

Toppenish

Toppenish, founded in 1907, was formerly part of the land roamed by the Yakama tribe, who fished for salmon in the Yakima River and gathered roots in the grasslands. Horses arrived in the 1700s, and the region's tall bunchgrass slopes and river bottomlands were well-suited for supporting large herds. Chief Kamiakin was keeping thousands of horses in the area by the early 1800s.

In the late 1800s, Ben Snipes and Charlie Newell began running large herds of cattle and horses in the Yakima Valley. Snipes (the "Cattle King") lost so many cattle during the hard winter of 1862 that, reportedly, one could walk up the side of Klickitat Mountain on their carcasses without touching the ground! Charlie Newell (1847–1932, age eighty-five), played a significant role in the area when, in 1884, he embarked on an impressive journey, driving seven hundred horses from the Toppenish area all the way to Kearny, Nebraska (Kearny was a crucial transportation hub, connecting the West to the rest of the country). By driving these especially hardy horses to Kearny, Newell facilitated trade and communication between the regions. The horses Newell transported played a crucial role in four wars: the Spanish-American War, the Philippine-American War, the Boxer Rebellion and World War I.

Today, almost nine thousand people call Toppenish, the "City of Murals," their home.

MARY L. GOODRICH LIBRARY

Reports suggest paranormal activity on the closed second floor of the 1921 Mary L. Goodrich Library in Toppenish. Rumors of strange noises, cold spots, books flung off shelves by unseen hands and footsteps from invisible people abound. Driving by, some have seen a female apparition standing in the windows on the second floor—which is always locked and unoccupied!

The former Yakama Indian Agency building was constructed in 1921 as a one-story structure. Seeing the need to start a small-town library, the citizens pulled together and gathered up $750. The City of Toppenish soon got involved and established a permanent library for its citizens in 1922.

Later, in 1931, a second story was added to the building. It was designed by Yakima architect John W. Maloney in an adapted Classical Revival style. This addition served as the Federal Indian Bureau's point of liaison with the Native American Yakama Nation.

After 1946, the building sat empty for a few years but then was sold to the local school district and used as a junior high school until 1954. That same year, the city purchased the library's current building from the Yakama Nation and transformed it into a bigger library; later, in 1976, a museum of local history was added. The library joined the Yakima Valley Regional Library System in 1980 and was later annexed in 2001.

Another interesting part of the building's history: there was once a prison cell in the basement used by the Office of Indian Affairs. If those walls could talk!

Although some claim Mary never worked at the library, it is interesting to note that Mrs. Mary L. Goodrich *was* listed as the librarian in the 1930 Toppenish city directory. Her husband, Levy J. Goodrich, worked at the First National Bank in town on West 1st Avenue, and in 1911, Mary was listed as a cashier at the same bank.

Perhaps she is the ghost that hangs out at the library? If not, then who is the female ghost that hangs out on the second floor? A different former employee? A local who loved the library and never wants to leave?

No one knows.

NOTES: The library is situated at 1 South Elm Street, Toppenish, Washington 98948.

The area has a rich history, and today, Toppenish is known as the City of Murals, with more than seventy-five paintings adorning its buildings, depicting scenes of the region's past from between 1840 and 1940.

GOLDENDALE

THE STONEHENGE OF MARYHILL

Good roads are more than my hobby, they are my religion.
—*Sam Hill*

Nestled near the Columbia River in Maryhill, there is a full-scale replica of Stonehenge built by Samuel Branson Hill (1857–1931, seventy-four years) as a memorial to World War I soldiers.

Above: Many feel Maryhill's Stonehenge in Goldendale, a replica of England's, is a conduit for paranormal activity and restless spirits. *Courtesy of LOC #2018698602, Carol M. Highsmith, photographer.*

Right: Some believe the spirit of Sam Hill (pictured here in his early thirties) haunts Goldendale, where he dreamed of creating a Quaker colony and his concrete mansion is now a museum. *Sketch drawn by Gabrielle D. Clements (1858–1948), courtesy of John E. Tuhy, via Wikimedia Commons.*

Some people believe that the site is haunted or has mystical properties, which has contributed to its legend. Spiritualists have been known to conduct ritualistic gatherings and hold special events at the site, and some claim the structure even contains a strange energy vortex.

But who was this man who created such a painstakingly bizarre version of the original Stonehenge in England—and a concrete mansion? Sam Hill was an adventurous and remarkable businessman, lawyer, railroad executive and financier who had a bit of a flair for the extravagant. He also became a well-liked advocate for the development of good roads in Washington State, among many other prosperous endeavors he pursued.

In 1879, Sam graduated from Harvard University and returned to Minneapolis (where he lived previously with his family) to practice law. He quickly caught the attention of James Jerome Hill (1838–1916, age seventy-eight), the "GNRR Empire Builder," who died with a fortune of about $63 million dollars (equivalent to about $1.6 billion today!). James Hill eagerly hired Sam to represent and protect his Great Northern Railroad Company from any possible fiascos. In 1888, Sam married into big money by wedding Mary Hill (no relation), daughter of a railroad tycoon—the powerful and very wealthy James Hill.

Sam, a Quaker, fell in love with the Columbia Gorge area (then just called Columbia), and in 1907–8, he purchased 5,300 acres of land. His dream was to create a Quaker colony there. He lovingly named the parcel Maryhill (after his daughter and wife, both named Mary). Sam formed the Maryhill Land Company and built a general store, a post office, a Quaker church, an inn and a stable with a blacksmith's shop.

Next, in 1914, he began building a fabulous concrete mansion in an old-world style. After some marital troubles, he realized the mansion would never be used as his personal residence, as his wife and daughter did not want to live at Maryhill. Construction of his mansion halted in 1917. (It was finally partially finished in 1940; the project was not completed in his lifetime).

Hill didn't know what to do with the building, and his beautiful female friend American dancer and entertainer Loie Fuller (1862–1928, age sixty-six) convinced him to use the vacant mansion as an art museum. In 1926, Queen Marie of Romania (1875–1938, age sixty-three) dedicated the new museum. (Fuller had introduced Sam Hill and Queen Marie at the 1919 Paris Peace Conference, and the three became acquainted on Hill's many trips to visit Europe.) Impressively, Queen Marie granted $1.5 million worth of paintings and statuary for the museum's Romanian Room! (Around $2.7 million in today's money.) She also donated some of her jewels and a cown for display. The museum also acquired original Auguste Rodin sculptures. Oddly, it also holds over one hundred chess sets in its collection!

Sam Hill also built a concrete Stonehenge replica at Maryhill that commemorates the dead soldiers of World War I. Hill had visited the original Stonehenge in 1915 as a guest of the British secretary of state for war, Lord Horatio Klitchener, and was fascinated by it.

It took his crew eleven years to build the Maryhill Stonehenge, but Hill was adamant about finishing. He engineered his personal Stonehenge much like one would a modern road, using slabs of reinforced concrete. Hill built it the way that he imagined the Druids would have if they'd had modern technology: uniform concrete blocks with an artificially imperfect exterior, all mortared into impressive megaliths. A bizarre task—but it still stands today as a testament to those who sacrificed their lives for the United States.

If one were to weigh all the pieces of this fake Stonehenge, they would come to about two million pounds! Countless people come from all over to gather at the Maryhill Stonehenge to celebrate the summer solstice, the "Hengestock" celebration, and Armistice Day. A nearby bronze plate

Orbs and strange lights have been witnessed near Sam Hill's grave in Goldendale. Many believe this is proof that Sam Hill haunts his beloved spot. *Courtesy of MagicalT, 2013, via Wikimedia.*

commemorates the fallen soldiers from Klickitat County who served and died between 1917 and 1918.

Sadly, the legendary and eccentric Sam Hill became sick and soon succumbed to intestinal influenza and a ruptured abscess in his stomach. He died in 1931 in Portland, Oregon, on his way to address the Oregon legislature in Salem, Oregon on behalf of the Good Roads Association He is buried below his beloved Stonehenge replica. Six years after Hill's death, his good friend Alma de Bretteville Spreckels (wife of San Francisco sugar magnate Adolf Spreckels) continued the process of turning the mansion into a museum, but it did not open to the public until 1940.

Some say they have seen mysterious orbs and flashes of lights near Hill's grave on the hillside near his Maryhill Museum. Does Sam Hill haunt his favorite place, the lovely hill where he once dreamed of a quiet existence with his family and his hoped-for Quaker colony?

NOTES: Stonehenge and the Maryhill Museum are located at 35 Maryhill Drive, Goldendale, Washington.
Directions: Take I-84 exit 104 in Oregon. Cross the river into Washington on Highway 97 and drive two and a half miles until it dead-ends at Lewis and Clark Highway/Highway 14. Turn right, drive one mile, then turn right onto Stonehenge Drive. Drive three-quarters of a mile; Stonehenge is on the right.

The twelve men honored by Sam Hill's Stonehenge are: Henry Allyn, Charles Auer, Dewey V. Bromley, John W. Cheshire, William O. Clary, Evan Childs, James D. Duncan, Harry Gotfredson, Robert F. Graham, Louis Leidl, Carl A. Lester, Edward Lindblad, Henry O. Piendl and Robert F. Venable. Rest in peace.

THE MURDER OF ANDREW BOLON

The life and times of an Indian agent in the late 1800s were extremely dangerous and unpredictable. One agent, Andrew Jackson Bolon (1826–1855, age twenty-nine), was just starting his married life when his life was tragically taken from him. He had only been working as an agent for two years, and his young wife was pregnant at the time of his brutal murder.

Some claim to have seen glowing orbs hovering over the monument that was erected in Bolon's honor at Goldendale, Washington. Perhaps Agent Bolon still wants people to remember his life and his service to the

United States? Perhaps he is hoping his skeleton will finally be found and peacefully put to rest?

Bolon came to Vancouver, Washington, by wagon train in 1845. He fell in love with and married Ms. Jerusha Short in 1849, when he was twenty-three years old. The two lived happily and peacefully together. They had a son named William (who unfortunately died at age two) and a daughter named Josephine. His wife, Jerusha, was pregnant again when Bolon took to the mountains on horseback—the last time she would see her husband alive.

In 1855, Bolon was proudly appointed Indian agent for all the Indians located east of the Cascade mountains. A Spokane Indian had secretly revealed to Bolon that several Yakama Indians had butchered six gold prospectors along the Yakima River, and Bolon was assigned to investigate the murders of those men.

On September 18, Bolon headed out to speak with Yakama chief Kamican (also Kamikan) about the killings. Several people strongly warned Bolon that Kamican would not hesitate to kill him when he arrived at his camp. But Kamican's brother, a man called Ice, was a friend of Bolon's—giving Bolon a false sense of security. As a friend, Ice also warned him of the wrath the chief could unleash if provoked. But Bolon had his job to do, so he pressed on.

When Bolon encountered a group of Natives, he felt they seemed friendly enough. But one of them quickly blamed Bolon for the hangings of several members of their tribe. This infuriated the chief, and he produced several hand signals: Bolon was to be killed!

Since Bolon could not speak their language or understand their hand signals, he was completely unaware of the doom that was about to fall on him. As the group stopped for the night to rest their horses, a hot fire was quickly made to get the men warmed up and start preparations for dinner. They were settled about nine miles north of Goldendale, in a beautiful spot near the George Garner cattle ranch. All seemed well, until…

As Bolon sat warming his cold hands, several men quickly jumped on him and slit his throat. Bolon did not even have a chance to fight back, and he bled out almost immediately.

Word went out that Bolon had been killed, but no one would reveal who his killer—or killers—was. Sadly, Bolon's daughter, named Anne, was born just three days after her father was murdered.

During the investigation, Bolon's body was never found. What happened to it? Where was it buried? All that eventually came to be known was that the Natives buried him somewhere near the water between Yakima and Goldendale. His corpse has never been unearthed.

Indian agent Andrew Jackson Bolon was only twenty-nine years old when his life was tragically taken in 1855. His body was never found. *Drawing courtesy of author from unknown photographer, 1850, via Wikipedia, uploaded by BlueSalix, 2014.*

The ruthless murder of young Bolon brought on much anguish between the United States government and the local Indian tribes.

Years later, an old Indian named Sul-lil (also known as Yakama George and Su-el-lil) wanted to set the record straight about Bolon's murder. Now seventy-six, Sul-lil was just a young warrior at the time he witnessed the murder with his own eyes. He told local rancher and reporter Lucullus Virgil McWhorter that a group of Natives under Chief Moshale (also Mo-sheel) had been responsible for Bolon's murder. He claimed that Moshale himself slit Bolon's throat as revenge for the hanged members of his tribe. Bolon's horse was shot dead and his body and personal effects burned. Then Chief Moshale stuffed Bolon's bloody, charred remains inside the hollow of an old tree. Sul-lil later led investigators to the exact spot where he saw Bolon had been killed, but no skeleton was ever located.

No one really knows the truth about what happened that tragic day, only that a young man in the prime of his life, with a lovely daughter on the way, was brutally killed—without any proof that he was responsible for any of the hangings.

Bolon's spirit lives on in the memory of his final days, a testament to the brutal fighting between men during the Indian Wars in the United States.

In 1918, two monuments were placed by the Washington State Historical Society in honor of brave Indian agent Andrew Bolon. The first monument was erected where Bolon's life was tragically taken (on land then owned by Wells Gilbert), in the presence of George H. Himes (secretary of the

Left to right: George Hines, Hazard Stevens, W.T. Bonney, Lucullus McWhorter and William Charley at the Andrew Bolon monument in Goldendale in October 1918. Stevens died the next day. *Courtesy of WSA.*

Oregon Historical Society), General Hazard Stevens (who was a good friend of Bolon's), W.T. Bonney (secretary of the Washington Historical Society), Lucullus McWhorter and Klickitat tribesman William Charley—who all unveiled the monument.

A second (and larger) Andrew Bolon Monument was placed in Goldendale, with his sad story forever etched into the granite.

NOTE: The Andrew Bolon monument is located on Upper Monument Road, about twenty-four miles outside of Goldendale. The monument marks the site where Andrew Bolon was killed by renegade Yakama in 1855. The monument was erected by the Klickitat County Pioneer Association and was restored in 2006.

To learn about other United States Indian Agents who were killed in the line of duty, please visit https://www.odmp.org/agency/3958-united-states-department-of-the-interior-bureau-of-indian-affairs-office-of-justice-services-us-government. The Officer Down Memorial Page Inc. (ODMP) is a nonprofit organization dedicated to honoring America's fallen law enforcement officers.

May their souls rest in peace.

Hanford

HANFORD GHOST TOWN

Hanford, Washington, is famous for its role in the Manhattan Project, which developed the atomic bomb during World War II (1939–45). The area around Hanford is said to be haunted by the spirits of workers who suffered radiation exposure and of those who died in accidents during the project. Some people claim to have heard strange sounds and seen apparitions in the ghost town of Hanford.

The small town was settled in 1907. The locals lived there peacefully, without much excitement, until 1943, when the United States government decided to bulldoze almost everything in sight. The residents of White Bluffs, Hanford and the surrounding areas were forced to sell their land and leave the area in just thirty days in order to make way for the upcoming Manhattan Project.

This top-secret project aimed to develop the first atomic bomb through the extraction and use of rare plutonium. (A few years later, this substance would also be used in the Trinity nuclear test.) During WWII, over fifty-one thousand people actively worked at the Hanford site. Grateful for the work, they had no idea of the personal risks involved.

But in 1949, things would get even worse for those involved in the project. In an operation classified as the Green Run, a large amount of radioactive iodine was released into the air. Why? To evaluate the ability of the U.S. Air Force to actively detect radioactive material if the Soviets were to release it in the United States. But this experiment would put the lives of countless people at risk as the radiation was intentionally distributed in the air over various populated areas. (It has since been determined that these chemicals concentrate in the thyroid gland, causing thyroid disease, among other complications, in those exposed.) To make matters worse, Hanford has estimated that over 440 billion gallons of radioactive waste were dumped into the ground, and they traveled through the soil and eventually entered the groundwater.

Hidden from the public for years, the research was kept secret—but several deaths and countless health problems brought light to the victims exposed to the toxic chemicals. Green Run remained a top government secret until the 1980s, when reports were finally made public in response to the many Freedom of Information Act (FOIA) requests.

Even today, people are concerned about the long-term effects of the Manhattan Project and Green Run on the environment.

It is no wonder the area may hold strange paranormal activity! The site is now one of the three Manhattan Project National Historical Parks and offers tours and valuable information.

NOTE: For more information and extensive collections of photographs, oral histories and more about the Manhattan Project and Hanford, please visit the Hanford History Project website at http://www.hanfordhistory.com.

PROSSER

STRAND HOTEL

Opened in 1910 as the Palace Hotel in Prosser, this building was once a bustling lodging house. After many prosperous years, the hotel was eventually in dire need of repairs and updates.

And, of course, it is haunted.

Some believe the ghost is called Carl, a former manager of the Strand.

Built in 1910 by George and Viola Bell Finn, the hotel has been a long-standing icon in Prosser. The building originally housed the Palace Hotel and was also home to businesses such as the Benton County National Bank, Pat's Cigar Store, Brockhausen & Hoch Grocery and Arends Bakery.

In 1935, the thirty-seven-room, twelve-bathroom hotel was managed by Mr. G.R. Halman, a man from Great Falls, Montana. Then, in 1938, a man named A. Carlino ran the Strand Hotel, acting as proprietor.

During World War II (1939–45), the Strand Hotel took on a new role, becoming a dormitory for female employees working on the DuPont Corporation's top-secret plutonium extraction project at nearby Hanford. (See "Hanford" on page 139.)

During the war, in 1941, the Strand Hotel went up for sale, its owner desperate to sell both the hotel and all its furnishings.

In 1956, Viola Bell Finn died at age eighty-four. She had been a Prosser resident since 1904.

By 1963, Fred Hall and his wife had run the Strand since 1948 (fifteen years), and they were ready to retire. It had transformed into a forty-room hotel with two apartments and living quarters for the owners. The hotel was again put up for sale, for a mere $16,000 (this deal also included all the furniture).

It appears many people called the Strand Hotel their home over the next few decades. Slowly, locals died in the hotel, leaving behind their beloved building—and possibly their ghostly spirits within its walls. In 1971, Jefferson Hyde, an employee of the Strand, died at age sixty-five. That same year, a young woman who lived at the Strand and her boyfriend were driving away from the hotel when they mysteriously crashed. Luckily, no one was killed. In 1974, Mrs. Frances Muns, who lived at the Strand, died. In 1984, a man named Carl Hayes, age seventy-eight, died. He also lived and possibly worked at the Strand. Could this be the Carl that the ghost is named after? Does Carl refuse to leave his favorite haunt?

Beautifully surrounded by vineyards, the hotel offered allure for entrepreneurs, and in 1985, an adventurous couple named Mike and Koni Wallace decided to remodel the place and open up the hotel as the Harvest House Bed & Breakfast. Mike was a winemaker, and his family owned the nearby Hinzerling Vineyards. The revised hotel would perfectly cater to the locals and entertain tourists.

But the Wallaces soon noticed objects moving on their own, doors opened and closed by phantom hands, chairs rearranging themselves and the sound of heavy footsteps walking down the halls. They felt the most paranormal activity occurred in the room that was once occupied by Carl. Maybe Carl's spirit has decided to stay at the Strand and watch what the future holds for his old stomping ground?

It is interesting to think of all the people who are connected to the Strand Hotel (also once called the Finn Building). It has housed various businesses over the years and will probably continue to do so for many years to come. We will have to wait and see if Carl continues to hang around!

GRAVITY HILL

One of the most bizarre areas in southeastern Washington is a section of road called Gravity Hill. Some people think the place is haunted by supernatural forces, which causes objects to move in the wrong direction. Could this really be true?

141

These unusual and unexplained experiences have been blamed on everything from aliens to ghosts to energy vortexes!

People have claimed that if they park their car on the road—located about fifteen miles north of Prosser—and put it in neutral, the car will magically roll uphill! (Someone has spray-painted a line on the road marking where the "weirdness" begins.)

But some say the strangeness is actually just an optical illusion. Or is it?

Locals offer that the nearby grain elevator is haunted, too!

There are several other bizarre places around the world that also seem to defy gravity: Mystery Spot in Santa Cruz, California; Spook Hill in Lake Wales, Florida; Gravity Hill in Arkwright, New York; Colina Gravity Hill in León, Mexico; Peanut Street in Belo Horizonte, Brazil; and Moncton Magnetic Hill in Moncton, New Brunswick.

NOTE: Gravity Hill is located approximately fifteen miles north of Prosser at 101204 North Crosby Road.

PASCO

THE HAUNTED MOORE MANSION

Now an incredible event center for weddings and celebrations, the lovely Moore Mansion is a three-story neoclassical estate located on the banks of the Columbia River in Pasco. It was built by prominent Seattle developer James Alexander Moore (1861–1929, age sixty-eight) for his wife, Eugenia Genevieve Jones (1867–1908, age forty-one). This fantastic property stretches two miles along the picturesque Columbia River and was once surrounded by over twenty thousand apple trees and seven thousand more various fruit trees.

Some believe the mansion is haunted by Mr. Moore himself, but since he never actually lived at the estate, the idea of him wanting to haunt it may be a little far-fetched. Or could it be that because he never got to enjoy the mansion while alive, he does so now, from beyond the grave? Another eternal mystery!

Moore did not have the easiest life and suffered much personal loss throughout his youth and marriage. Originally from Nova Scotia, Canada,

Right: A rare picture of James Moore. His fabulous mansion in Pasco now serves as a beautiful event center. *Drawing courtesy of the author, based on brochure* Seattle and the Orient *(1900), courtesy of Wikimedia.*

Below: The dark figure that is seen casually roaming the Moore Mansion is a friendly and helpful ghost, so there is no need to be scared! *Courtesy of Wikimedia, by Allen4names, August 2012, public domain.*

he moved to New York as a young man. He married Genevieve in 1885 in Denver, Colorado. Together they had several children, but tragedy would strike the Moore household. In 1872, his brother George passed away at age five. His mother, Isabell, died in 1892. Next his son Horton passed at just two years old. His sister Helen was called away in 1897, followed by his father, Andrew, in 1899.

After all this loss, the Moores moved to Seattle in 1900 and began their new life together. Moore became fabulously wealthy by developing high-end (still existing) neighborhoods such as Capitol Hill and Green Lake. A grand estate was built with their fortune on Seattle's Capitol Hill (it still stands today).

Sadly, Genevieve contracted tuberculosis, and her health began to fail. The family physician suggested a better climate might help Genevieva's lungs heal. Moore quickly commissioned the construction of the Moore Mansion in Pasco, in hopes that the drier weather would be beneficial in the recovery of his beloved wife. But tragically, the disease won, and his wife of twenty-two years passed away in Seattle. She never got to enjoy living in the fabulous estate he had built for her.

After her death, the mansion sat vacant for many years, until 1914, when a meat-packer from Tacoma, Washington, purchased it.

Moore moved to Florida from Seattle to continue his lucrative real estate developments. In 1916, he married Elsie Clark, and the two went off to New York together to start their new life. After a few years, the couple moved to the warmth of San Francisco, California.

Moore never returned to the mansion in Pasco. During Prohibition (1920–33), the estate was turned into a speakeasy.

In 1929, Moore succumbed to myocarditis (inflammation of and damage to the heart muscle) and pericarditis (inflammation of the pericardium, a thin membrane around the heart) and passed away at the Palace Hotel in San Francisco with Elsie at his side. His friends and family believed that he actually died from exhaustion and overwork, as Moore was never one to sit still.

In 1948–49, the Pasco area flooded, causing much damage to the mansion and surrounding buildings.

In the 1950s, the estate was transformed once again, into a nursing home. In 1979, the Pasco mansion was added to the National Register of Historic Places.

Today, the fabulous estate has been painstakingly restored to its former glory and can be rented for special occasions, events and weddings.

The dark figure that is seen casually roaming the Pasco mansion remains a mystery to employees. Most consider the spirit a friendly and helpful ghost, so there is no need to be scared!

PROSSER

ST. MATTHEWS EPISCOPAL CHURCH

The St. Matthew's Episcopal Church in Prosser has received a good amount of attention due to its haunted nature. Paranormal activity has been documented and recorded there by the crew of TV's *Ghost Hunters* series (season 3, episode 16, 2006–07). Church members called in the *Ghost Hunters* crew because of the number of unexplained phenomena they had been witnessing: the odor of burning wood, the apparition of a boy ghost and a strange phantom size 6 footprint left for all to see.

The church's chancery (its administrative office building) was once a mental institute for children that burned down and was rebuilt. Could a tragic fire have caused the residual energy that creates the odor of burning wood from the past?

NOTE: The St. Matthew's Episcopal Church is at 317 Seventh Street, Prosser, Washington 99350.

WALLA WALLA

The history of Walla Walla is rich and fascinating, with roots that stretch back centuries.

Near the mouth of the Walla Walla River, where Lewis and Clark camped in 1806, their expedition encountered the Walla Walla people, as well as the Cayuse, Umatilla and Nez Perce tribes.

In 1818, the Northwest Company established Fort Nez Perce to trade with Native American groups. In 1821, the fort was acquired by the Hudson's

Postcard of Main Street, downtown Walla Walla. In 1847, a dark, tragic massacre occurred in Walla Walla, which is home to several notorious spirits. *Courtesy of SPL #5568.*

Bay Company and renamed Fort Walla Walla. It served as a major stopping point for migrants moving west to Oregon Country.

In 1831, Nez Perce delegates embarked on a two-thousand-mile expedition to St. Louis, seeking information about the "Great Father" and Christianity. This journey sparked a personal interest in Marcus Whitman (1802–1847, age forty-five), a doctor and Protestant missionary, which led to the later arrival of the Whitman group in the area in 1836. The group's ultimate goal was to convert any and all local Indians to the Christian faith.

Upon their arrival, Whitman established a mission in Oregon Country for the Walla Walla tribe, which played a crucial role in the region's early settlement. Unfortunately, the idea of converting the local tribes did not go as smoothly as planned. (See "The Whitman Massacre," page 150.)

The 1860s gold rush brought a surge of settlers to the area.

By the 1880s, Walla Walla had become the largest city in Washington Territory due to its growing agricultural industry. The fertile land supported many orchards, hops fields and vineyards.

The town was incorporated and named the seat of Walla Walla County in 1862. It continued to thrive as a hub of commerce, culture and education. Today, Walla Walla offers a blend of history, wine country and vibrant community.

KIRKMAN HOUSE MUSEUM

The second-oldest brick residence in Walla Walla and one of Northwest's most admired Victorian structures is the beautiful Kirkman House, built in 1880. The Italianate Victorian was the home of William Kirkman (1831–1893, age sixty-two) and remained in the Kirkman family for three generations. At one time, the home was going to be demolished and turned into a parking lot! Luckily, it was saved in 1977, when the home was purchased by the Historical Architecture Development Corporation. In 1975, the building was added to the National Register of Historic Places.

Now the estate is a museum—and the former Kirkman family refuses to leave their beloved mansion! Many have seen Mr. Kirkman himself peering from behind curtains or roaming the halls. Other family members join in on the fun, and their apparitions can be seen wandering in and out of the rooms. Perhaps the Kirkmans just enjoy reliving their past while

The historic Kirkman House is now a museum, and it is well known that the former Kirkman family refuses to leave their beloved mansion! *Courtesy of LOC #2018699167, Carol M. Highsmith, photographer.*

museum directors and volunteers retell the history of the prominent Walla Walla family.

William Kirkland came from Bolton, England, and when he was twenty-one years old, he moved to Boston, Massachusetts. The following year, he moved to sunny California for a brief period. The years 1853 to 1862 found him in Australia, but then he moved back to California.

Kirkland made his money dealing with cattle, and he drove herds from California to Idaho with his partner John Dooley. The team became financially successful.

He met Isabelle Potts (1845–1931, age eighty-six), and the two were married in 1867 in San Francisco. The couple moved to Walla Walla in 1866 and decided to make the city their permanent home. The Kirkmans became incredibly involved in the community. Sadly, only four of their ten children survived to adulthood: William, Fanny, Myrtle and Leslie. (Fanny's room is one of the most paranormally active in the museum.)

The Kirkmans suffered personal heartache when six of their children died either at birth or very young. But the family continued to support and promote Walla Walla for twenty-one years, making many good friends and acquaintances.

Unfortunately, while the family was traveling back from England in 1893, William died unexpectedly of neuralgia of the heart while on a train in Stevens Point, Wisconsin, at age sixty-one.

The citizens of Walla Walla mourned deeply, and flags were hung at half-mast. The funeral was held at his residence on Colville Street in Walla Walla. So many citizens showed up to pay their respects to Kirkman that they flowed from the house out into the yard and street.

Perhaps the man who loved Walla Walla for twenty-one years enjoys hanging around his beautiful home, remembering the life he once lived with his adoring family.

Their beautiful family headstone at Mountain View Cemetery in Walla Walla reads, "To live in hearts we leave behind is not to die."

NOTE: The Kirkman Museum is located at 214 North Colville Street, Colville, Washington 99362. The museum hosts fun events such as ghost tours, murder mysteries, children's activities and Victorian Christmas and is also available for weddings and meetings.

MARCUS WHITMAN HOTEL

One of the more notoriously haunted buildings in Walla Walla is the Marcus Whitman Hotel. Built in 1928 in the Renaissance Revival style by architect Sherwood Ford, the structure has many unique features.

Some paranormal investigators consider the Whitman Hotel the most haunted place in the state! Both visitors and employees have witnessed many ghosts and heard unexplained noises.

One of the more familiar ghosts is called the Woman in White, although nobody seems to know who she was or why she hangs around the hotel. Possibly the spirit goes back to an earlier time, prior to the construction of the hotel? Do ghosts necessarily have to hang around in a specific location? Can they travel to various sites, much as they did while living? Some paranormal researchers say yes.

Some paranormal investigators consider the Whitman Hotel the most haunted place in the state! One of the more familiar ghosts is called the Woman in White. *Courtesy of Phbludwig, 2012, via Wikimedia Commons.*

NOTE: The Marcus Whitman Hotel is located at 6 West Rose Street, Walla Walla, Washington 99362. The thirteen-story, 133 room hotel is named after Protestant missionaries Marcus (1802–1847) and Narcissa (1808–1847) Whitman, who settled and built a mission near Fort Walla Walla in the vicinity of a Native Cayuse settlement in 1836.

The Marcus Whitman Conference Center is located at 107 North Second Avenue in Walla Walla and occasionally conducts ghost tours. Its doors have welcomed such guests as the twenty-seventh United States president, William Taft (1857–1930) in 1911; the thirty-fourth U.S. president, Dwight Eisenhower (1953–1961) in 1954; and *Batman* actor Adam West (1928–2017).

THE WHITMAN MASSACRE

Marcus (a doctor and Protestant missionary, 1802–1847, age forty-five) and Narcissa (1808–1847, age thirty-nine) Whitman came to the Walla Walla area by covered wagon in 1836 with a fellow missionary couple, Henry and Eliza Spalding. Narcissa was born in Prattsburgh, New York, and always dreamed of becoming a missionary. Unfortunately, during that era, a woman could not follow her calling if she were unmarried. After quickly falling in love, Narcissa overcame the obstacle of being single by marrying Dr. Marcus Whitman on February 18, 1836, in Angelica, New York.

The Whitmans embarked on the journey of a lifetime with the hopes of establishing a mission in Oregon Country and converting the Cayuse Indians to Christianity. Their mission played a crucial role in the region's early settlement. After a grueling expedition, they finally arrived at Fort Walla Walla on September 1, 1836. Narcissa and Eliza would go down in history as the first documented European-American women to cross the Rocky Mountains.

Since Marcus was a physician and Narcissa was a chemistry teacher, the duo felt they had much to offer. The couple tried extremely hard to live among the Cayuse, and they eagerly provided food and education to them. They even adopted several children and welcomed them into their family. Their own daughter, Alice (1837–1839), died tragically in the Walla Walla River when she was just two years old. Narcissa took great pains to teach the Cayuse women how to bake, iron, wash and mend clothes, clean thoroughly, make soap and do other valuable domestic chores.

When an outbreak of measles tore through the area, Marcus and Narcissa did everything they could to combat the horrible epidemic. Unfortunately,

In 1847, the brutal Whitman massacre by the Cayuse tribe shocked the community. Over a dozen people were killed, including Marcus and Narcissa Whitman. *Engraving by Nathaniel Orr & Co., 1877, public domain, via Wikipedia.*

their efforts were in vain, and sadly, over two hundred local Cayuse tribe members died. This did not sit well with the Cayuse.

Since many of the White settlers somehow survived the outbreak, the Cayuse became suspicious and accused the doctor and his wife of being murderers—of poisoning the Cayuse in order to steal their land.

On November 29, 1847, the Cayuse instigated a horrible attack against the Whitmans and other missionaries as the group relaxed inside the Whitmans' modest home. Marcus suffered a fatal tomahawk blow to his skull. The cruel murder of the lovely Narcissa quickly followed, as well as the brutal killing of eleven others. Narcissa was the only woman to be massacred that horrible day. A local warrior, Frank Escaloom, shot her under her left arm. As she lay bleeding to death on a settee, she could hear the moans of her dying husband but was unable to help him.

Narcissa would be the target of two more bullets, one to her cheek and another to her body. At just thirty-nine years old, Narcissa Whitman would die at the hands of the very people she had tried so desperately to help.

This tragedy could have generated residual energy, which might explain the paranormal activity. Perhaps Narcissa herself is the lovely Woman in White that people see roaming the glorious hotel? Her spirit could be restless for good reason. Betrayal, anger, pity, horror—all are emotions that can trap

Above: The graves of Marcus and Narcissa Whitman at the Whitman Mission Cemetery which marks the location of the Waiilatpu Mission in 1836, which ministered to the Cayuse Indians. *Image courtesy of* The Columbia River: Its History, Its Myths, Its Scenery, Its Commerce, *by W. D. Chapman, 1909, public domain.*

Left: Is Narcissa Whitman the Woman in White who haunts the Whitman Hotel? Perhaps the hotel being named after her family causes Narcissa to hang around. *Drawing based on descriptions of Narcissa, courtesy of the National Park Service, public domain.*

a victim in time and space, unable to move on to another dimension. Or perhaps she is just honored a hotel is named after her family and happy that they are not forgotten by history?

NOTES: The Whitmans are buried at the Whitman Mission Pioneer Cemetery, located at 328 Whitman Mission Road, Walla Walla, Washington 99362.

The people massacred in 1847 were Marcus Whitman, Narcissa Prentiss Whitman, Andrew Rogers Jr., James Young Jr., Lucien Saunders (schoolmaster), Nathan Kimball, Mr. Osborne (carpenter), Crockett A. Bewley, Isaac Gillen, John Sager, Francis Sager, Mr. Canfield (blacksmith), Jacob Hoffman, Mr. Marsh, Amos Sales and Jacob D. Hall. Rest in peace.[*]

For a detailed account of the massacre and its aftermath, please discover an engrossing read titled "Whitman Massacre: The Aftermath" at http://www.oregonpioneers.com, compiled by Stephenie Flora, at http://www.oregonpioneers.com/whitman3.htm. The site also contains detailed personal information regarding the dozens of others who were killed or survived the tragedy on its "Roster of Victims of the Massacre" page: http://www.oregonpioneers.com/whitman4.htm.

FORT WALLA WALLA

Fort Walla Walla is rumored to be haunted by soldiers from wars past. Claims of ghostly figures, moving objects and bizarre and unexplained sounds are experienced on the grounds and inside the buildings.

There have actually been four Fort Walla Wallas! (Of which only the fourth and final one remains.)

The first fort was a small fur trading post built in 1818, where the Columbia and Walla Walla Rivers meet. The Nez Perce would trade their furs for blankets, pots, guns and other necessary items. But it was not long before problems began to arise between the soldiers and the local Natives, causing the fort to be closed in 1855.

In 1856, the second fort was built (just a few miles from where downtown Walla Walla is today), but it closed within one year.

The third fort was built to house troops and stable the men's horses. A fine officer's quarters was also constructed. None of these buildings remain today.

---

[*] Information from William McBean, *Oregon Spectator*, December 10, 1847.

Fort Walla Walla, Wash.

1638.

8433.

Fort Walla Walla is haunted by soldiers from wars past. Ghostly figures, moving objects and unexplained sounds surround the grounds and buildings. *Postcard courtesy of Brück & Sohn, 1906, public domain, via Wikimedia Commons.*

Steptoe Butte is over four hundred million years old and 3,612 feet above sea level, offering breathtaking panoramic views of the surrounding countryside. *Courtesy of SPL #4104, Thomas White Tolman (1851–1935), photographer.*

The fourth and final fort was built in 1858–59 to house the soldiers who fought in the Pacific Northwest Indian Wars. Lieutenant Colonel Edward Steptoe was in charge of the troops. (This is the fort that resides today at the present site. An incredible fifteen of the original buildings still stand on the property.)

In May 1858, Steptoe led 159 soldiers and Native American scouts to Fort Colville, and the battle was on! Over one thousand Natives from multiple tribes attacked Steptoe and his men. Two officers, one Indian scout, four soldiers and an unknown number of Indian warriors were killed.

The Fort Walla Walla cemetery was established in 1856, and buried there were many of the soldiers tragically killed in the Indian Wars. In 1877, the commanding officer's house was built, as well as multiple barracks over the next few years.

In 1902, the Ninth Cavalry, a famous unit of buffalo soldiers, which had 16 White officers and 375 Black soldiers, was stationed at the fort. The troops used the fort continually until 1905, then the Fourteenth Cavalry served at Fort Walla Walla until 1908, primarily stationed there to maintain law and order. The fort was finally shut down in 1910. When the Saint Mary's Hospital facility was completely destroyed in a fire on January 27, 1915, the fort was turned into a makeshift hospital.

In 1917, the world would be forced into action during World War I, and 260 men trained at Fort Walla Walla, preparing for battle.

Another horrible fate awaited the United States in 1920, threatening the lives of countless people. Tuberculosis was rampant, and Fort Walla Walla was converted again to a hospital and was renamed the Jonathan M. Wainwright Memorial VA Medical Center.

It is unknown how many people died at the fort during the epidemic. Any number of patients who passed on the grounds could be the spirits that remain on the property!

Today, the fort is a fascinating and educational museum. Spend the day touring the historic structures and remember and honor all the men and women who served our country. The museum features a fantastic seventeen-building historic pioneer settlement, five exhibit halls, an old jail cell and dozens of fun activities and events.

NOTE: The Fort Walla Walla Museum is located at 755 Northeast Myra Road, Walla Walla, Washington 99362.

LIBERTY THEATER

More than moviegoers take a seat in the beautiful Liberty Theater in Walla, Walla. It is reported to be haunted, and several paranormal investigators have evidence of unusual activities.

Designed by Henry Osterman and Victor Siebert, the theater opened its doors to the public in 1917 as the American Theater. It entertained the public with silent movies and live music, and people could sit in luxury in the one thousand mahogany and Spanish leather seats. The owner, Arthur W. Eiler, prided himself on offering such a fine space, and in 1922, he installed an expensive organ to accompany the silent movies. Eiler was also an avid fisherman and would often entertain visitors by telling his fishing tales.

Although no one knows who is haunting the theater, it is interesting to note that the site where it stands was originally old Fort Walla Walla in 1856 before the fort was moved in 1858. Perhaps any hauntings are due to activity at the fort and not the theater? It remains a mystery.

As of this writing, the theater is undergoing remodeling and updating, and hopefully it will be open for everyone to enjoy again soon.

NOTE: The Liberty Theater is located at 50 East Main Street, Walla Walla, Washington 99362.

The beautiful Liberty Theater is reportedly haunted. It opened its doors to the public in 1917 as the American Theater. *Courtesy of LOC #2017708124, John Margolies, photographer.*

Dayton

One of the more notorious buildings in Dayton, located thirty miles from Walla Walla, is the old Weinhard Building. One of Dayton's finest businessmen, Jacob Weinhard (1849–1941, age ninety-two) was born in Stuttgart, Germany, and arrived in the United States in 1870 when he was just twenty-one years old. He quickly went to work for his uncle, the famous maltster Henry Weinhard (1830–1904, age seventy-four), in Portland, Oregon, who owned the Liberty Brewery (renamed the City Brewery in 1862).

Jacob developed a love for beer making and quickly learned the craft himself. Recognizing the fabulous barley-growing potential of Columbia County, he believed it was an ideal place to start his brewery. He decided to move to Dayton in 1880 and brought several types of barley seeds with him. First he opened his own brewery, the Jacob Weinhard Brewery, then an opera house and the Fountain Saloon, on the corner of Front and Main Streets. He married Caroline Giebenhain (1860-1930, age sixty-nine) in 1881, and they proceeded to have eight children. Jacob built the Weinhard Building in 1890

Three rooms at the Weinhard Hotel are haunted. Room 16 has a female ghost, 11 has unusual activity and noises and room 12 has moving objects. *Courtesy of publichall, April 4, 2006, via Wikimedia Commons.*

The marvelous Henry Weinhard Brewery in Portland, Oregon, was quite a sensation in 1890, producing four thousand barrels of beer that year! *From a "New Year's Greeting" ad in the* Morning Oregonian, *January 1, 1914, public domain.*

(which is now the Weinhard Hotel). The Weinhards became prominent in Dayton, and everyone loved them.

Jacob retired from the beer business in 1906. The Weinhards lived a peaceful life in Dayton for many years. Caroline died in 1930, and Jacob never remarried. He died in his home after a lengthy illness.

The hotel is said to have various paranormal activity, all of which is friendly. Some claim room 16 holds a young female ghost. Room 11 is said to have unusual activity and phantom noises. Room 12 has been associated with objects moving and a depression appearing in the bed when no one is lying there. No one knows who the spirits are at the Weinhard Hotel.

NOTE: The Weinhard Hotel is located at 235 East Main Street, Dayton, Washington 99328.

PULLMAN

WASHINGTON STATE UNIVERSITY: STEVENS HALL

Stevens Hall at Washington State University (WSU) has been part of countless students' lives since it opened its doors in the summer of 1895.

Elizabeth Duncan holding a black cat similar to the one that has haunted Stevens Hall since the 1900s. *Courtesy of LOC #2018709092, Arnold Genthe, photographer, 1926.*

It is the oldest residence hall and the second-oldest building still standing on the campus. Named after Isaac Stevens, the first territorial governor of Washington, this historic hall has a rich and varied architectural style. It was made from locally sourced materials, including brick, basalt, Puget Sound fir and red cedar shingles.

Numerous halls at State College of Washington (now WSU) have unexplained paranormal activity. Many students and staff members have witnessed ghosts and heard strange noises. *Courtesy of LOC # 2013646958, 1909.*

And its many spirits roam all over the university!

The building is haunted by a girl who walks up and down the halls. Rumors suggest a young woman lost her life in Stevens Hall and it is her spirit that haunts the building. Several of the other buildings on campus are known to house a few ghosts, too.

But not all ghosts are people; they can be animals, too. Students claim they see the spirit of a large black cat that roams the campus—a legend that dates back many years. During the early 1900s, Stevens Hall was a bit of a social hub. Everyone would gather to read books together, enjoy tea and even hold dances. One fun tradition was for the students to gather on Halloween night and read Edgar Allen Poe's story "The Black Cat." Legend says that the students noticed a black cat just outside of the dorm mother's room one night. They knew that black cats were considered bad luck, but they paid no mind to such silly ideas. Unfortunately, they found their dorm mother dead the next day! Was it the curse of the black cat that killed her or natural causes?

Other stories tell of a mysterious dark flying object that lives in the attic, frightening students half to death. Since these ghost stories have been retold

for so many years and students keep experiencing strange paranormal activity, there can be no doubt that someone or something is haunting Stevens Hall!

ORTON HALL

Orton Hall at WSU was built in 1959 and can house about 350 students—plus a friendly ghost. The legend of Railroad Sam still scares and delights students up for a good fright. This ghost is said to linger around the Orton Hall dormitory. One might be inclined to think that Railroad Sam was the victim of a tragic accident involving a train, but that is wrong. It was his love of trains that earned him the nickname! His ghost is said to stand near windows and stare out into the streets. Most people who have witnessed Railroad Sam's ghost say his appearance times itself perfectly with the passing of a train. Who is this male entity? No one knows. Since the campus has been around since 1895, the spirit could be any number of people who have lived in Pullman over the past one-hundred-plus years.

BRYAN HALL

The 1909 Bryan Hall is one of the oldest buildings on campus. Designed by architect J.K. Dow, it is named after Enoch A. Bryan (1855–1941, age eighty-six) who served as the college president of WSU from 1893 to 1915. Its distinctive and beautiful clock tower makes the building easily recognizable. Since 1909, countless students and staff have enjoyed its beauty. Over the years, it has hosted notable speakers, including President William Howard Taft, Booker T. Washington, Helen Keller and even President John F. Kennedy. The clock tower has been adorned with crimson-colored neon lights since 1946. The original clockfaces were in continuous use from 1910 to 2010. (In 2010, the old wooden faces were replaced with new steel ones.) The tower is truly a work of craftsmanship. It reaches one hundred feet up into the air, and the four clocks are each a whopping ten feet wide.

Bryan Hall is said to be haunted by late college president Enoch Bryan, and his favorite rocking chair in the attic moves on its own. *Courtesy of LOC #2016860776, Harris & Ewing, photographer, 1905–45.*

Bryan Hall is said to be haunted by Enoch Bryan, who was a remarkable man with a fascinating life. Born on May 10, 1855, in Bloomington, Indiana, he was the son of a preacher. He attended Indiana University Bloomington, earning a bachelor's degree in 1878 and a master's degree in 1884. Later, in 1893, he obtained a master's degree in classical studies from the prominent Harvard University. (He continued his education with doctor of law degrees from four collages: Monmouth College, Michigan State University, Indiana University and Washington State University.)

In 1893, Bryan arrived at Washington State University, and by 1894, he had assembled a diverse faculty, covering fields from English to agriculture, horticulture and engineering.

Bryan set a clear academic direction (combining liberal arts with practical education), a legacy that endures to this day. In 1905, he successfully advocated for changing the institution's name to Washington State College to reflect its broad range of studies.

Bryan was a well-loved and highly respected man who played a significant role in defining WSU's future. After many years of devoted service, Bryan died in Pullman on November 6, 1941. He was buried on November 8 in the Fairmount Cemetery in Pullman, alongside his daughter Bertha, who died in 1900, and his wife, Hattie, who died on November 26, 1935.

It is said that Bryan's favorite rocking chair is in the attic, and it moves on its own, as if Bryan still enjoys sitting in it. It is reported that when he was alive, he loved to share a good ghost story. Perhaps it is not a stretch, then, to believe it is Bryan himself who haunts his glorious hall.

THE GHOST OF PERHAM HALL

A tragic "young love gone wrong" story took a fatal twist just before Christmas break in December 1980. While many were planning their fun holiday vacations, an eighteen-year-old boy was plotting something very sinister.

John Stickney (who lived on Mercer Island, Washington, and worked in Monroe, Washington at a rock quarry as a chuck tender) could not manage the breakup of his three-year-long relationship with a student. Their on-again, off-again affair was over for good, as far as the female student thought.

But John just could not take no for an answer.

On the seventeenth of December, John made the long drive to Pullman with the high hopes of rekindling their broken relationship. He arrived too late to meet up with his ex-girlfriend, so he stayed the night and tried again to meet up with her later the next afternoon. Around three o'clock, he arrived at the dormitory with a large duffle bag in hand. Inside the bag were multiple explosives.

After the girl refused to listen to John, he must have shown her the bag's contents, because she and her roommate immediately ran out of the building, warning everyone else to head to the safety of the backyard. Once notified, two brave officers quickly tried to calm John down and get him to drop the battery pack that would allow him to detonate his homemade bomb. John refused to listen. In a blink, the bomb went off, killing John instantly and seriously wounding several others, including Corporal David Trimble.

Several of the walls on the fifth floor of the six-story concrete Perham Hall building were destroyed. The lives of almost fifty students were put at risk, and the damage cost the college $150,000. Luckily, no other persons were killed in the bombing, but many people's lives were changed forever that evil day.

Perhaps John's ghost is wandering lost, seeking forgiveness for his actions. Perhaps he is still searching for his lost love. Perhaps he is just restless and cannot move on to the other side...

IN CONCLUSION

I hope you have enjoyed reading about all the wonderfully haunted places and strange occurrences in Eastern Washington. Perhaps these stories and legends will inspire you to take a fun road trip and see many of these places for yourself! These local tales of intrigue and horror are designed to pique your wild imagination while sneaking in a little bit of the history of the buildings and early pioneers of each town.

So again, thank you to all my followers, editors and friends. Without your interest and support, my books would not be possible.

Happy ghost hunting!

Spirit photographs were published in the late 1800s for both amusement and profit. *Courtesy of LOC #2022647935, Melander & Bro., publisher, 1875.*

BIBLIOGRAPHY

Articles

Ayer, Tammy. "That's the Spirit: Yakima's Haunted Past Only Adds to Supernatural Beauty." *Yakima Herald-Republic*, May 20, 2017.

Ferolito, Phil. "Is the Toppenish Library Haunted?" *Yakima Herald-Republic*, October 30, 2016.

Flora, Stephenie. "Whitman Massacre: The Aftermath." OregonPioneers.com, 2004. http://www.oregonpioneers.com/whitman3.htm.

Foster, Drew. "Which Way Is Up?" *Tri-City Herald*, June 21, 2009.

Kershner, Jim. "Tales from the Morgue." *Spokesman Review*, October 31, 1999.

Klein, Christopher. "America's First UFO Sighting." History.com, updated January 15, 2020, originally posted November 9, 2016.

Klein, Sandor. "Saucers Are Real, Spotter Insists." *Spokane Chronicle*, November 18, 1957.

Metcalf, Gale. "Is the Harvest House Haunted?" *Tri-City Herald*, June 23, 1985.

Meyers, Donald W. "It Happened Here: Ben Snipes Builds Ellensburg's First Bank." *Yakima Herald-Republic*, August 7, 2022.

———. "It Happened Here: History Passed through Yakima Train Depot." December 10, 2017.

———. "It Happened Here: Stagehand's Ghost Haunts Capitol Theatre." *Yakima Herald-Republic*, October 24, 2021.

Nath, Anita. "Wenatchee Incorporates as a Fourth-Class City on January 7, 1893." HistoryLink.org, October 23, 2009.

Van De Venter, Karlee. "Gravity Hill Has Stumped Experts for Decades." *Bellingham Herald*, May 24, 2023.

Washington State University. "Our Story: Campus Legends and Ghost Stories." http://wsm.wsu.edu/ourstory.

Wikipedia. "List of Lake Monsters." https://en.wikipedia.org.

Wilma, David. "U.S. Army Colonel George Wright Hangs Yakama and Palouse Prisoners at the Ned-Whauld River Beginning on September 25, 1858." HistoryLink.org, January 29, 2003.

Books

Moffitt, Linda. *Washington's Haunted Hotspots*. Atglen, PA: Schiffer, 2009.

Woog, Adam. *Haunted Washington*. Guilford, CT: Morris Book Publishing, 2013.

Newspapers

Adams County News (Ritzville, WA)
February 9, 1898

Colfax (WA) Gazette
October 9, 1908

Columbian (Vancouver, WA)
December 28, 1994

Corvallis Gazette-Times (Albany, OR)
July 31, 2005

Courier Herald (Kennewick, WA)
October 14, 1937

Ellensburg (WA) Dawn
October 7, 1909

Evening Statesman (Walla Walla, WA)
June 7 and 8, 1905
June 13, 1905
June 22, 1905
June 26, 1905

Goldendale (WA) Sentinel
October 10, 1918

Kansas City (MO) Times
October 26, 1893

Longview (WA) Daily News
October 31, 2009

News Tribune (Tacoma, WA)
May 11, 1904

Olympian (Olympia, WA)
October 31, 2009

Pullman (WA) Herald
June 30, 1893
April 21, 1904
May 7, 1904
July 2, 1904
December 30, 1905

Sacramento (CA) Union
July 3, 1938

Seattle (WA) Post Intelligencer
April 26, 1893
October 18, 1893

October 21, 1893
February 7, 1898

Spokane (WA) Chronicle
January 8, 1898
June 7, 1905
January 2, 1906
August 31, 1906
October 2, 1908
August 2, 1952
November 18, 1957

Spokane Falls Review (Spokane, WA)
April 11, 1889
September 26, 1890
June 19, 1945

Spokane (WA) Press
November 12, 1921
April 12, 1923

Spokesman Review (Spokane, WA)
April 23, 1891
June 2, 1893
October 18, 1893
December 20, 1897
June 28, 1902
March 10, 1904
June 14, 1904
June 28, 1904
October 3, 5 and 9, 1909
October 29, 1918
November 27, 1918
June 17, 1919
November 27 and 28, 1924
January 1, 1936
April 1, 1937
October 30, 2009

Tacoma (WA) Daily Ledger
January 20, 1890
April 26, 1891
June 24, 1893
April 13, 1897
March 22, 1898
October 6, 1918

Tacoma (WA) Times
February 7, 1898
June 22, 1904

Tampa (FL) Times
January 31, 1980

Times News (Twin Falls, Idaho)
January 31, 1980

Tri-City Herald (Pasco, WA)
July 7, 1963
June 22, 1996

Wenatchee (WA) Daily World
January 7, 1909
December 22, 1910

Wichita (KA) Eagle
June 22, 1996

Yakima (WA) Herald
January 30, 1890
April 8, 1897
April 26, 1905
January 22, 1908
December 16, 1908
September 8, 1909
July 20, 1910
October 26, 1910
May 31, 1911

Websites

Ancestry. https://www.ancestry.com.

Find a Grave. https://www.findagrave.com.

GhostQuest.net. http://www.ghostquest.net.

Hanford History Project. http://www.hanfordhistory.com.

Haunted Places. https://www.hauntedplaces.org.

HistoryLink.org. https://www.historylink.org.

Legends of America. https://www.legendsofamerica.com.

Library of Congress. http://loc.gov.

National UFO Reporting Center. https://nuforc.org.

Paranormal Catalog. http://www.paranormalcatalog.net.

Wikimedia. https://www.wikimedia.org.

Yakima Valley. https://www.visityakima.com.

INDEX

ABOUT THE AUTHOR

Originally from Ithaca, New York, Deborah Cuyle loves everything about the history of America's cities—large or small. She is currently living in a haunted, crumbling mansion that was built in 1883. Even creepier? It was once used as a funeral home. The home has three resident ghosts—all of whom are friendly!

Deborah loves to sit and share ghost stories with anyone who will partake. A big fan of exploring, one never knows where Deborah will end up next!

ALSO BY DEBORAH CUYLE

Ghosts and Legends of Northeast South Dakota (SD—coming soon!)
Ghosts and Legends of Spokane (WA)
Ghosts of Coeur d'Alene and the Silver Valley (ID)
Ghosts of Leavenworth and the Cascade Foothills (WA)
Ghostly Tales of Coeur d'Alene (ID)
Ghostly Tales of Snohomish (WA)
Ghostly Tales of the Pacific Northwest (OR, WA and BC)
Haunted Everett (WA)
Haunted Snohomish (WA)
Haunted Southwest Montana (MT)
Images of Cannon Beach (OR)
Kidding Around Portland (OR)
Murder and Mayhem in Coeur d'Alene and the Silver Valley (ID)
Murder and Mayhem in Deadwood (SD—coming soon!)
Murder and Mayhem in Spokane (WA)
The 1910 Wellington Disaster (WA)
Wicked Coeur d'Alene (ID)
Wicked Spokane (WA)